YOUR FAMILY
HISTORY

By the same author

WORDS WORDS WORDS

HOW SURNAMES BEGAN

HOW PLACE-NAMES BEGAN

Lutterworth Press

ENGLISH SURNAMES

PLACE-NAMES OF THE ENGLISH-SPEAKING WORLD

Weidenfeld & Nicolson

HAILEYBURY SINCE ROMAN TIMES

Privately printed

YOUR FAMILY HISTORY

And How To Discover It

C. M. MATTHEWS

Revised edition

LUTTERWORTH PRESS
GUILDFORD SURREY ENGLAND

First published 1976
Reprinted 1977
Revised edition 1982
Reprinted 1983

ISBN 0-7188-2542-X

Printed and bound in Great Britain at
The Camelot Press Ltd, Southampton

To the memory of a very special aunt

MARY CARRINGTON

(1849–1940)

who first taught me to care about my ancestors

Contents

An eight-page section of monochrome plates appears between pages 64 and 65.

Abbreviations

The following abbreviations are used in the text:

BM   British Museum

CRO   County Record Office

DNB   Dictionary of National Biography

GLRO   Greater London Record Office

MI   Memorial Inscription

PCC   Prerogative Court of Canterbury

PR   Parish Register

PRO   Public Record Office

Acknowledgments

The author and her publishers wish to express their thanks to Miss M. E. Holmes, County Archivist of Dorset, and to the staff of the Dorset County Record Office in Dorchester, for their generous help in the obtaining of the photographs.

Our thanks are due to the following, who gave permission for the photographing and reproducing of documents and registers:

The Rector of Hazelbury Bryan, for Plates 1 and 3
The Vicar of Gussage All Saints, for Plate 2
The Rector of Melbury Osmond, for Plate 4
The Dorset County Record Office for Plate 5
Colonel Sir Joseph Weld, Lord Lieutenant of Dorset, for Plate 6
Lady Teresa Agnew, for Plate 7

We are also grateful to Mrs Pamela Burgess-Green, for permission to use in Plate 8 the gravestone photograph which was Plate 18 in her late husband's book, *English Churchyard Memorials* (Frederick Burgess, Lutterworth Press, 1963).

The author would also like to express her gratitude to Mrs Sarah Barton for her help.

I

How To Begin

One sometimes hears it said that So and So belongs to 'a very old family'. This is nonsense for of course all our families are equally old. The difference lies only in the fact that some people have their family history well-preserved in old records and know a lot about their ancestors while others know very little; but for them too the relevant records may exist and could perhaps be found if properly searched for.

Detective work is always intriguing and what can be more fascinating than trying to unravel one's own private mystery? I say 'trying' because no one can be certain of much success. There is a lot of chance in it as well as hard work. One enthusiast may remain baffled in spite of perseverence while another strikes a rich vein of information that leads on and on. Another warning to the beginner is that once you find a few clues you may get so bitten with the bug of genealogy that you can never stop. For however much you find out you will always want more.

The difficulty for most people is to know how to set about it.

In the search for ancestors each of us starts with a piece of personal equipment that will make an enormous difference to our progress at every turn—our surname. This is one of the ways where luck comes in, for a rare surname is a constant help, but if you have a very common one your chances of following your family far are slim unless you know that they lived in a small community where they can be safely identified. Even then if you lose the thread it will be hard to pick up again.

Fortunately our family background offers a choice of surnames. Our grandparents usually provide four different ones and each earlier generation doubles the number. Some enthusiasts try to follow all the lines as far as possible, others prefer to concentrate on one, but if you are stuck you can always try another, and those with the more unusual names will probably be the most rewarding.

Apart from the fact that a rare surname helps you to identify your own forbears among a mass of names, surnames are full of interest in themselves, and many of them give a strong indication as to the part of the country where they originated. A very large number of them consist of place-names. They may not always be easily recognised as such, partly from the vagaries of spelling over the centuries (Lester, for instance, is just a simplified spelling of Leicester) and sometimes because the place itself is obscure and little heard of. But every surname derived from a place-name does signify that your forbears once lived in that spot.

If your name does not obviously belong to a different type—that is to say, it might be a descriptive word like Short, or Whitehead, or tell of an occupation such as Baker, or the father's Christian name as Jackson—if in short it has no recognizable meaning, then it is always worth looking for it in a gazetteer of the British Isles. The gazetteer must be a big one that gives all kinds of places, for the name in question could be derived from that of a river, a wood or a district as well as a town or village. It could come from a farm or a field name and then you are unlikely to find it; but it is worth trying.

Of course it may happen that there are several places of this name. Bartholomew's Gazetteer, for instance, has over two columns each of Nortons and Suttons (north and south village) and that will be no help at all in locating a family. But if you find your name occurring in just one district you may be pretty sure that the first of your ancestors to be called by it came from there.

However that was a long time ago, probably six or seven hundred years, for the majority of English surnames were firmly established before 1400. And although your ancestors may have stayed in that region for centuries, perhaps moving no more than a few miles from their name-place, yet they may equally well have migrated to some other part of the country and done it so long ago that the clue afforded by the place-name is of little practical use. None the less it is of interest. It spurs you on. It gives a point to aim at. And if you can follow your family back from their more modern haunts to somewhere nearer their name origin you will enjoy a great sense of achievement.

Apart from giving actual place-names there are other ways in which surnames can direct you to this or that part of England or, of course, to

Wales, Scotland or Ireland. This is a complex subject and will be more fully discussed in Chapter 13. And it must be stressed that at best these indications of locality, intriguing though they are, are apt to point to something far off. The immediate business of genealogy is not to speculate about remote origins, but to start with what we know for certain—which is often not more than two or three generations—and from there to work back, step by step into the past, establishing each foothold firmly as we go and hoping that from it we will see the way to the next.

How much is known to start with varies widely from one family to another. A great many people are familiar with their grandparents, have a vague idea of a great-grandfather and after that a total blank. Others are much better informed but often what they have been told is vague and woolly, and for them too, sooner or later comes the blank. The first thing to do is to collect every relevant fact, particularly dates, names in full and addresses, beginning with those you can be sure of, at least a generation before the blank.

This sounds almost too obvious to be worth saying, but it is surprising how many items of useful information may exist unknown to you among your own possessions or those of your relations and how helpful they can be to your researches. Feeling suddenly curious about your family history you may rush to London and spend hours searching for your grandfather's birth in the General Register Office (see page 21) only to fail through lack of preparation. Later on at home when clearing out some old books you may see on the fly leaf of one, '*To my dear godson, George Augustus Matthews, on his tenth birthday, May 5th, 1875.*' There is the exact date you are needing, not to mention the second name that George had carefully suppressed. Armed with these facts you will easily obtain the birth certificate that will lead you back to the previous generation.

Go through old letters, diaries, albums, newspaper cuttings, books, and anything that may have inscriptions. It used to be the custom to enter personal history in the family bible and where these have been kept they can prove invaluable. Visit churchyards and study tombstones. Try everything.

Most important of all, get every item you can from your oldest relations. Old aunts and—better still—great-aunts can be rich mines of family lore. In earlier generations women were more at home than men and the details of family life were often their main interests. You may have found their anecdotes boring in the past and paid scant attention, but now listen carefully, ask the right questions and have patience. Don't hustle the old dears but try to keep them to the point.

'Do you know where your father was born?'

'Of course I do, dear. He took me there to show me when I was quite a little girl. Such a pretty place.'

'What was its name?'

'Let me see. I remember it had a very nice church. My father used to sing in the choir.'

Just wait for it. It may make all the difference to your success to have the name of that village. And when she has gone it will be gone too, unless you can get hold of it now.

Then there are cousins as possible informants. They may never have shown any interest in the family but they are descended in part from the same ancestry as yourself. They may have inherited old papers unknown to you or scraps of family tradition different from those that you have heard. My husband knew that his maternal ancestors came from Kent but failed for years to locate them. Then on a trip abroad he met a second cousin in Fiji who told him of a village where some of them were buried. On our return we went there and found some splendid tombstones ('splendid' because their inscriptions though old were legible) and a succession of entries in the parish registers giving a line of solid yeomen back to the reign of Elizabeth I. He could have written to that cousin years before, but had never thought of it.

Next think what local records may be available in the district where your family lived. Many provincial newspapers are old foundations going back to the early nineteenth century. You can find their addresses in telephone books and either ring or write to ask how far their files go back and when it would be convenient for you to see them. If you know when your grandfather (or other forbear) died, you may find an announcement of his death or perhaps an account of the funeral and something useful may come to light, or something unexpected.

Or perhaps, if you know his profession or place of employment, there will be some institution or business concern where he worked that is still in existence. If so, you can write to it asking for any record of him that they may have, such as his age and address when first he joined them. Or you may have heard of a school or college that he went to and these may still exist and have old records.

Or maybe the local library has some old directories from which you can find out where your family was living a hundred years ago or even longer.

Kelly's Directories for towns and counties began publication in 1845 and there were others before that. If you can't find one of the period you want you can write to Kelly's own reference library which houses the complete series (see page 134) and will answer postal enquiries as to whether particular names are included, giving details.

If your ancestors were sufficiently distinguished you can of course consult various standard works such as the full edition of the *Dictionary of National Biography* or some of the large volumes on the nobility and gentry by Burke or Debrett. These can be found in any good reference library; but if your family branched off from the main line a long way back you will want early editions (Burke's *Landed Gentry* for 1837 is specially useful) or the volumes on extinct or dormant titles, and for books of this sort you will need to go to a really big library. Sooner or later your research is bound to take you to one of the great national libraries and of these something will be said in Chapter 8. In the meantime check whatever can be checked in your own neighbourhood, assemble facts and traditions, and make yourself a firm platform from which to launch out.

As to those aristocratic origins spoken of by your grandmother, they may be genuine but more remote than she suggested. It is enjoyable to establish a real link with a family whose descent is recorded in one of the official books of genealogies. It is like a lucky throw in Snakes and Ladders by which you are suddenly taken on through several generations without any labour on your part. But to make such a connection every step must be properly checked, with no gaps or guesswork, and the only way to do it, as with more ordinary ancestry, is to start with what you know yourself and work back.

2

Keeping Your Records

As you collect material you must write it down and it is most important to do this intelligently from the start. Many people, including myself, have started off on the genealogical quest with boundless enthusiasm and lack of method, making every mistake possible before learning the hard way.

Professional genealogists have devised various ways of setting out their findings, but I would say that no very elaborate method is needed provided you do have a method and stick to a few basic rules. Always write down anything that could possibly be of use *at once* as soon as you find it or hear it. Don't rely on your memory, thinking that you will write it down when you get home. Don't write on loose sheets of paper, unless they are the sort to be incorporated immediately into a proper loose-leaf folder. Don't write in any old notebook you may happen to have that already has notes on other subjects in it. If you are anything like me you will lose some of the loose sheets, mislay those scrappy notebooks and waste endless time later on hunting for items which you are sure you copied out 'somewhere'. Of course if something comes up unexpectedly you will use the back of an envelope or whatever comes handy, but copy it out carefully into a proper notebook the first moment you can.

Start with at least two good-sized, well-bound notebooks. You can get more as required, but two will do for a start. Keep one for setting out the principal facts in their proper order, **with the source of each fact beside it.** In this book it can be put very briefly; the full details, taken down directly from the source, will be in one of the other books.

I have found it a good method for this my principal notebook, which I will call Volume I, to allot a double page to each individual forbear as far as I know them, with hopeful spaces for more as my knowledge extends. (A few blank pages at the beginning will be useful too.) I head each right-hand page with the name in full if I know it, and the relationship to an earlier established person, as *My father's father*. Under this I write the headings, *Birth, Marriage* and *Death*, suitably spaced out, and fill in the basic details as far as I can. Between these there will be room for entering other facts such as education, appointments and achievements, all with dates if possible. The same method will apply however remote the ancestor. For your parents and grandparents you can be selective, putting down only the principal facts, but further back where your knowledge is scanty write in anything that could be useful, with details of how you know it.

For the generation nearest to you, you may be so sure of the facts from first-hand knowledge that a tick can indicate that this is so, but before you tick anything ask yourself 'Do I really know that is true?' For even one step back sources of information become extremely important and must always be given. For instance under *Marriage* you would ideally give the exact date and place, followed by the letters *P.R.* (Parish Register), or *G.R.* (General Register) which would mean that either you or someone you trusted had seen the official record, or you might write *Cert.* if you have the certificate. Alternatively your source may only be Great-Aunt Deborah. This may turn out to be perfectly accurate, but if it doesn't lead to anything it may become suspect and should be checked.

On the opposite page I write any further details about the source and possible methods of procedure. For instance if all you could enter for your great-grandfather's marriage was *In Ipswich about 1830. (Great Aunt Deb.)*, you may add on the opposite page *She was very positive* or *a bit uncertain*; and later on you may have to write *Not in registers of St Peter's or St Lawrence's. 1825–37 both searched. Try other parishes* (Ipswich is a town full of old churches). This brings up another important rule. **Always keep notes of what has been searched even if nothing useful is found.** Elimination may be disappointing at the time but it is a step forward none the less. It at least prevents your going over the same ground twice.

Eventually if you do track down the marriage in Ipswich you can write in the details of exact date and place (including the parish) on the right-hand page, giving Aunt Deborah a grateful thought, for without her you would probably never have found it. But on the bridegroom's page I put no more about the bride than her name, for her details must go on her own page (and if she was married in her own home parish it should now be fairly easy to find her birth and parentage).

Likewise the particulars of the children born to this couple will be on another page, or pages, too. You will already have allotted a page to the one from whom you are descended, and you may think that you only want to follow the direct line and not bother with uncles, great-uncles and so forth, but it is important to note the details of each generation if possible. The brothers and sisters can all go on one page if you like but record what you can of them. Their dates of birth can sometimes prove to be useful, and their Christian names in full can establish connections with earlier ancestors. They can even be of interest in themselves.

Under the heading *Death* you may be able to give the exact date and place, or perhaps you may have to begin with something vaguer such as *Dead by 1861. (Widow remarried. See next page.)* If you know where the person in question is buried be sure to put that down and indicate if there is a tombstone or other inscription to be seen by the letters *M.I.* (memorial inscription). And if you know of an obituary or account of a funeral in a newspaper you can give a reference to that.

Towards the end of this notebook I use some more double pages for family trees as they develop. Some day you will want to make a fair copy on a large sheet—perhaps one for each line of descent, showing as many generations as possible. For advice on this see Chapter 7. But before you are ready to do that you can make the first rough drafts based on what you know so far, and these are useful for showing relationships at a glance.

My second and subsequent notebooks are used for taking down information at source as it is discovered. As your researches depend partly on where you happen to be and what is available at one time and place (and in one library you may look up very different types of material) these notes will not be in any logical order. You can't carry a battery of notebooks and I often have just the current one with me. But I do number the pages and give cross-references to link items that reasonably should come together. In fact if several items, noted at different times, fit together nicely I copy their essentials jointly on to a fresh page. And any item that qualifies for Volume I is carefully written in.

I also give references from Volume I to the other notebooks. For instance, after giving the date of a death I may add *Buried; Combe Hay, near Bath. M.I. (See Vol. 3, page 14).* In Volume 3 the memorial inscription is copied out in full.

If in doubt whether some item you find has any bearing or not, always make a note of it 'just in case'. If it is long and you don't think it worth the trouble of copying you can summarise it very briefly and note exactly where you found it so that later on if it turns out to be significant you can find it again quickly without trouble.

To summarise my system: one book contains an orderly short statement of what is known of each individual, a sort of dossier where one can quickly see the gaps as well as the facts, and this is cross-referenced to the other books where all possible evidence is recorded fully. Some researchers prefer a card index to my first volume and there is a great deal to be said for it, for if somebody's page gets overcrowded or untidy it is good to be able to set it all out again on a new card. But every man to his own taste.

However you set about it, remember that the object of the enterprise is not only to put all the evidence down in such a way that you can easily find what is known about each person, it is also to be able to evaluate the evidence. Family tradition passed on orally is very important and should always be noted, but hard facts from official documents are even more so, and it must always be clear which is which. So always give your references, and in those later notebooks never write down anything without an exact heading saying what it is and where you found it. If it is in a large record repository, such as Somerset House, note its official reference number so that you can see it again easily if need be. It took me years to learn that.

Of course in writing your notes you will soon find yourself using abbreviations and this is one more matter that you had better clarify from the start. The best thing is to make your own list on one of those blank pages at the beginning of Vol. I, adding new ones as occasion arises. Do use the standard ones that are used by professional genealogists and compilers of reference books. There is generally a list of them with their meanings at the beginning of the book, as there is in this one. But also make up your own as required. I am lucky enough to have diaries kept by both my grandmothers in the 1840s, and when I use one of these as authority for a statement I write *D* (for Diary) followed by the appropriate initials. But if you use initials in this way be sure to list them at the beginning so that all is clear.

Even the simplest abbreviations can cause confusion at a later time if you aren't consistent. You might think that there could be no mistake about *b.* and *d.* standing for 'born' and 'died'. But if you are copying a number of items out of a parish register the words that you will keep seeing on the page before you will be *baptised* and *buried*. If you are anxious to get down as much as possible in a limited time you may easily write *b* for either of them, and you may also put *d* for daughter. It is true that the context will generally make the meaning clear, but mistakes are possible, and it is better to form the habit of writing *bap*, *bur* and *da* to make all clear. It is all so fresh in your mind as you write it you think you could never be muddled. But genealogy isn't all over in a few weeks or months. It is something you may lay aside for years and then take up again. And what about posterity? Don't write the kind of notes that only you can understand, and perhaps not even you for ever. I look at some of my early jottings now in despair, thinking 'What on earth does that mean?'

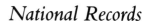

When you have assembled all the facts that can possibly be gleaned from your home, your relations and your local library, your next step depends largely on where you are. If you can easily visit the district where your immediate forbears lived you can get to work at once on local records, the chief of which will be the parish registers.

But if, on the other hand, you live far from the haunts of your ancestors or perhaps don't even know yet where they were, then your best policy will be to visit those great fountainheads of information in London, Somerset House and the Public Record Office, each of which has been much re-organized in recent years and has overflowed into new offices. What you learn at one of these is apt to send you scurrying to another, so it is fortunate that they are all close together.

For nearly 150 years the vital statistics of the nation, that is to say the births, marriages and deaths of England and Wales since July, 1837, were kept at Somerset House. But now the whole of this **General Register** has been transferred to St Catherine's House at the corner of Aldwych and Kingsway. You walk in from the busy street and find yourself surrounded, walled in as it were, by hundreds of great volumes. These don't contain the detailed records themselves but indexes to them, through which you may search freely for as long as you like. No ticket or fee is required, but you must pay for any certificate you ask for. A separate search room at Alexandra House, Kingsway, houses the indexes of deaths; but all certificates must be ordered at St Catherine's.

Let us suppose that you want to track down a great-grandfather who you think must have died in about the 1880s. You·have heard anecdotes about him and seen a photograph with splendid whiskers but you know few facts.

You want to find his parentage and background and the best way to start is by discovering how old he was at the time of his death.

Now is the time when the preliminary collection of facts at home comes into play and it is to be hoped that you have been able to narrow down that date of death as much as possible. The indexes were filled as the deaths occurred and each volume covers only three months. So even if you know the exact year you may still have to take down from the shelf, search and replace four volumes, and they are very heavy. Professional genealogists like to make jokes about the great muscular strength needed in their occupation, and it is a fact that if you have to look through five years of indexes (twenty volumes) your arms will be aching, ten years and you may feel exhausted, but it can be done.

Inside each volume the order is alphabetical, so each can be fairly quickly searched, but if the name is at all common you may have difficulty in identifying the right person. Within the whole population many people have identical names and even a name that is rare in the world at large may be common in one district. A distinctive second name is a great help or a knowledge of the place where the death occurred. The index gives four clues to identification: the name in full; the date of death, but only to within a quarter of a year; the registration district (a list of these is available in which you can look up villages to see which district would include them); and the age of the deceased, but this is given only after 1865. If you know even one of these things besides the name it may help you to select the right entry. You can then order a certificate and learn a little more.

If you are in doubt between two or more people with the right name and with possible dates, districts and ages, and if you know some definite fact (the exact date of death, the full address, the occupation), ask at the order desk. It may be possible for the authorities to check the possible entries against your extra information and ensure that you get the right certificate.

The certificate unfortunately tells you little more than what you have already discovered but probably enough to make it worth getting: cause of death, place of death more precisely than in the index, occupation, age and the name of whoever reported the death. This last is generally the nearest relative at hand, often the widow or eldest son or daughter, and these names can be useful in confirming that you have got the right person.

Probably the most important point for you to learn is the age, which, combined with the date of death, will give you the birth-date. As already mentioned the age is given in the index—but only after 1865. If your ancestor died before that date you will have to get the certificate, which causes some

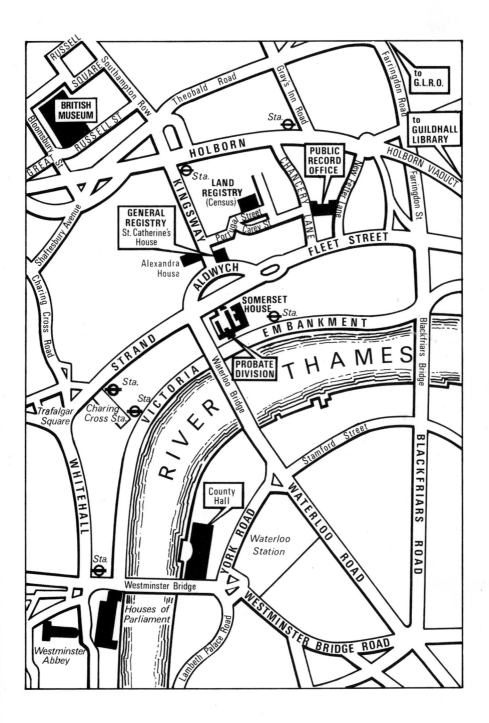

REGISTRATION DISTRICT Bath

1859. Birth in the Sub-district of Walcot in the County of Somerset

No.	When and where born	Name, if any	Sex	Name and surname of father	Name, surname and maiden surname of mother	Occupation of father	Signature, description and residence of informant	When registered	Signature of registrar	Name entered after registration
208	First January 1859 1 Walcot Parade	Charles Walter	Boy	Henry Edmund Carrington	Emily Frances Carrington formerly Jones	Proprietor	Emily H. Carrington Mother 1 Walcot Parade	Tenth March 1859	— Rigister	1

Registration District Bath[bridge]

1890. Marriage solemnized at the Parish Church in the Parish of St Mary the Less Bambridge in the County of Bambridge

No.	When married	Name and Surname	Age	Condition	Rank or profession	Residence at the time of marriage	Father's name and surname	Rank or profession of father
250	Sept 9th 1890	Charles Walter Leamington	31	Bachelor	Clerk in Holy Orders	[illegible]	Henry Edmund Leamington	Journalist
		Margaret Constance Pughe	28	Spinster		1 Belvoir Terrace Bambridge	Grange Pughe	clerk in Holy Orders

Married in the Parish Church according to the Rites and ceremonies of the Church of England by Banns by me

This marriage was solemnized between us,   Charles Walter Leamington   John J. H. Pughe   Philip
   Margaret Constance Pughe   in the presence of us,   Philip at Exeter   Vicar of Bambridge

REGISTRATION DISTRICT Trowbridge

1941. DEATH in the Sub-district of *Trowbridge* in the *County of Wilts*

No.	When and Where died	Name and surname	Sex	Age	Occupation	Cause of death	Signature, description and residence of informant	When registered	Signature of registrar
79	Thirtieth July 1941. Gen. Nore. Hospital Staverton R.D.	Charles Walter Carrington	male	82 years	Retired Mayor of Christchurch, New Zealand	1(a) Cerebral haemorrhage (b) Hypertension Certified by Beda H. Gidron, M.R.C.S.	C.E. Carrington, Son, 200 Evelyn Road, London N.W.1.	Thirtyfirst July 1941.	Charnad. Registrar

Shown here are copies of the birth, marriage and death certificates for Charles Walter Carrington. The entries in the indexes at St Catherine's for each certificate are as follows:

Births, March quarter, 1859   *Carrington, Charles Walter, Bath, 5c, 756*

Marriages, September quarter, 1890   *Carrington, Charles Walter, Cambridge, 3b, 930*

cross-referenced under the bride's name   *Pughe, Margaret Constance, Cambridge, 3b, 930*

Deaths, September quarter, 1941   *Carrington, Charles W., Trowbridge, 5a, 243*

In each case the penultimate number is that of the district and the last number is that of the relevant page of the register.

delay as either you must call for it, some days later, or have it posted which takes longer. But if the name you want appears in the index after 1865 you can by-pass the death certificate and, having made your calculation, proceed at once to the index of births.

Beginning now to feel like an old hand, you should find the birth easily, that is to say if its date is not too early. If you have found that your ancestor was born before 1837 you will have to pursue him elsewhere.

Another possible snag is that the age given on the death certificate isn't always totally reliable. The date of death must be correct as deaths had to be registered at once by law, but the age is more open to human carelessness. Members of the dead man's family would probably know it and give it correctly, but even they might be mistaken, and if his wife had died first and only a housekeeper was there to answer the doctor's questions as he filled in the form she might give her opinion which was no more than a guess, and the doctor put it down thinking it 'near enough'. So if you don't find the birth where it should be, just search a year or two in each direction.

The certificate will give you the address where the child was born, the full names of both parents, the occupation of the father and the maiden name of the mother, all leading usefully to another generation.

You may be able to go straight on to the marriage of these parents, and again an approximate date is what you need. If the great-grandfather whose birth you have just found was the eldest child it should be easy. But if you don't know his position in the family, and it may have been a large one, it could mean a long search and you might be able to use your time among the records better. It all depends on what you know and what you most want to know. The marriage certificate is especially useful as a pointer to the bride's family. (If you already know the bridegroom's surname and the bride's maiden name, cross-check in the marriage indexes; the reference number beside both names should be the same.) It gives the place of the marriage—usually her home parish—and the names and occupations of the parents of both bride and bridegroom. There will also be the names of the witnesses and the officiating parson. Note them all down. They may turn out to be of interest.

If you can't conveniently get to London you can apply for any of these certificates by post (see page 122). But it will take longer and cost more, and you will miss all the excitement of the search. Then again if you do it yourself you can note down various things that you happen to find without bothering to get certificates. You can in fact have a field day at little or no cost, provided your arms are strong enough.

It should also be pointed out that if you know for certain where that great-grandfather's birth, marriage or death took place you have the alternative of getting the details from the District Registry Office which may be more convenient for you. In this case it is cheaper to make the enquiry by post, giving what particulars you can. A search of up to five years will be made for you without charge, and you pay only for the certificates, but if you insist on going yourself you are charged for access to the indexes— this is just the opposite of the London procedure. However the wider scope of the London office is sure to tempt you there sooner or later.

Besides the records already mentioned the General Register Office has some military and R.A.F. records, registers kept by British consuls abroad since 1849, and those of births and deaths at sea since 1857.

It should be added that **certificates of entry** and **naturalisation papers** ('Home Office', HO) are at the Public Record Office at Kew (see below). Unfortunately, many people who came here in the last century (or'earlier) did not go through any legal formalities and so do not appear in the P.R.O. records; it is simplest to telephone Kew first, and enquire.

We must now think of the ancestor who was born before the days of civil registration, that is before July 1837. For him and those who went before him your main source will be parish registers. But if you don't know what parish he was born in, a good way to find out is by way of the 19th-century **Census Returns**. Copies of the relevant parts of these are now available on microfilm in most of the County Record Offices but the original returns for the whole of England and Wales are preserved in the **Public Record Office** (P.R.O.) in London.

The old main building of the P.R.O. is in Chancery Lane but like Somerset House it has overflowed and at the time of writing (1982) the Census Returns are housed in the Land Register Office in nearby Portugal Street (see page 23). There is also a large new Record Office at Kew, of which more later. For Chancery Lane and Kew, you need an official Reader's Ticket (the same one does for both), for which you should apply well in advance. However, if you only want to see the Census Returns, you can go straight to Portugal Street and sign in for a day there, without getting a reader's ticket first.

The first census in Britain was made in 1801 and since then there has been one every ten years, except during the last war. But the first three recorded only numbers, and that of 1841, though it does give names, is very short on further information. But those of 30 March 1851, 7 April 1861, 2 April

1871 and 3 April 1881*, are gold mines for researchers. Beyond that date they are not yet released.

To find a particular person in one of these returns you must know where he was living at one of these key dates. If he was in a village or small town its name will be enough, but for a large city you will need a more detailed address, with at least the name of a street or parish. Various indexes in the census room will help you to locate these within the city.

The need for an address may be a stumbling block, but if you have already seen the death certificate you will know where the person died, and he may have been living there for some years. Or you may be able to find his will, which should give his home address at the date it was made (probably several years before his death). And again, all that information you noted down from older members of your family should help. If you are stuck, try old directories (page 14). You must of course have some knowledge to start with, but if you know the town or the county a directory may give you further details. However it must be admitted that they tend to give only the more solid and well-established residents. People who moved about and lived in rented accommodation can be hard to locate.

If you have still no address for one of the vital census dates, a good way to solve the problem is through the next generation. Supposing it is a great-grandfather that you want to locate; do you know roughly when any of his children were born? If you think your grandparent or a brother or sister was born within a few years of one of those dates, you can find the birth certificate giving the place of birth, which was almost certainly their own home. And if, as you work hopefully through the birth indexes, you strike Great-Aunt Emily when you were aiming at Great-Uncle Horace it doesn't matter, provided you get that home address.

When at last you present yourself armed with an address for one of those census years you will find that modern methods are in use and instead of seeing the original document you will have it on microfilm. First—as in all record repositories—you must hunt through an index to find the code number for the part of the census you want, then at last comes the exciting moment when you are seated at the machine with the film in place. Instead of turning pages you turn knobs—nervously in my case, for supposing they had gone away on a visit that very week. Then suddenly, there it is, your great-grandfather's name in his proper place of residence, with all his household gathered about him. Here you will see his occupation, his and his wife's ages and the parishes where they were born. You will see the children that they had at that date, perhaps including some that you had

---

*Not released at time of writing (Jan., 1982) but due shortly

never heard of because they died young. There may be some other relative who lived with them, perhaps one of an older generation whose birth-place and date will help to take you back further. There may also be details of servants, which can give an idea of social standing and financial state of the family. Note everything. It may all come in useful. But above all make sure you have taken down accurately your ancestors' ages and the places where they were born.

It should be realized that the national record repositories mentioned in this chapter deal only with the records of England and Wales. For research of this kind into Scottish families you will have to go to Edinburgh unless you do it all by post. In such matters as registration of births, marriages and deaths Scottish law has always been independent of England and civil registration did not become compulsory in Scotland until 1855. But when it did more detail was required than in England which partly makes up for this.

These records are to be seen at the **New Register House in Edinburgh**. The **Census Returns** for Scotland are also kept there, and so are many old parish registers. Other records, such as wills and deeds, are at the **Scottish Record Office**. These important offices are very busy, especially in the summer months, so go prepared (see page 138). The Mormons have been allowed to film the pre-1837 Scottish parish registers, and the index to their researches (described in more detail on page 44) can be a great help.

Hunting Scottish family history has its own problems and some advantages. The best book on the subject is *In Search of Scottish Ancestry* by Gérald Hamilton-Edwards, or if you fail to find a copy of that, his more general book, *In Search of Ancestry* devotes two chapters to work in Scotland and lists other more detailed works that might be helpful. The same book has a useful chapter on Irish records.

In Ireland civil registration did not begin until 1864, and most of the census returns were destroyed in the disastrous burning of the Four Courts in Dublin in 1922. However, some Irish records remain, and addresses of the **Record Offices in Dublin and Belfast** will be found on page 139–40.

The facts that one gets from official documents are so plain and impersonal that one longs for some warmth and colour—just a few extra details to bring them to life, and the best hope of finding these is in wills.

All the wills of England and Wales since 1858 are available at the **Principal Probate Registry** at Somerset House. (For Scottish wills you will have to go or write to Edinburgh. See page 138.) The names of the testators are indexed in volumes which you may look through without charge, and if you find the name you want you may see a copy of the will at once for a small fee, or order a photocopy at rather higher cost. Most wills mention some relations, and give some idea of the person's tastes and occupation. Reading one is in fact a good way of filling out the picture of a Victorian ancestor of whom you knew few personal details.

It is easy to find the name you want in these indexes provided you have some idea of the date of death. Each volume covers one year, and even if you have to look through a good many years you will find it less arduous than doing the same thing in the General Register of deaths (as described in the last chapter) where each year occupies four volumes. For this reason some researchers use these indexes of wills for finding the date of a death. A good idea, provided the person in question made a will (not everyone did by any means) or had enough property to warrant a legal administration. Administrations (called Admons in the official lists) are included in the Somerset House indexes, but from these you get only a few bare facts such as the date of death and the name of the next of kin who inherits. Remember that although many widows and maiden ladies made wills if they had anything much to leave, married women did not do so before 1882 when the Married Women's Property Act came into force.

To find a will made before 1858 is more complicated, but it is easier than it used to be and well worth some trouble for the farther back you go the more fascinating the details when you find them, and the greater the likelihood of learning something new.

Two books have recently been published by leading genealogists, A. J. Camp and J. S. W. Gibson, each devoted to the subject of wills and how to find them. Mr Camp's book is slightly the more comprehensive of the two and Mr Gibson's rather easier for beginners but their scope is very similar. Even without them you can go ahead and look for wills by straightforward methods, but if you don't have much success either of these books, if you can see it in a library, should give you some further suggestions.

The first thing to grasp at the start of your quest is that wills were formerly under the jurisdiction of the Church and were proved in ecclesiastical courts. A man of modest means whose possessions were all in one place would have his will proved in the local archdeacon's court; if his property was more widespread it would go to the bishop's court; and if he had goods or land in more than one diocese it would be dealt with by the Prerogative Court of Canterbury (commonly known as the P.C.C.) or the equivalent for York, the P.C.Y. But if his property lay in both archbishoprics the P.C.C. had precedence. It followed that all the chief landowners and many prosperous merchants and tradesmen had their wills proved in these high courts, especially in the P.C.C., and as it then seemed that this was the proper thing to do a good many people who were not obliged to use this highest court preferred to make use of it, which they could do by paying the higher fee. Consequently the indexes of the P.C.C. which go right back to the 15th century contain a pretty fair record of the deaths of the heads of families of the upper classes.

At the time of writing (1982), these P.C.C. wills are at the Public Record Office in Chancery Lane, where you can see them, on microfilm, if you have a reader's ticket (page 27). Their indexes are printed up to 1700 and from 1853–58. For 1700–1852 there are the original handwritten indexes at the P.R.O. in which names were listed, year by year, under the surname initial only, as they came in. Searching them can be a long job. However, the Society of Genealogists (page 64) has a card index of P.C.C. wills from 1750–1800 and is in the course of publishing a full printed index from it. For the period 1796–1857, you can also try the indexes to the Estate Duty Registers at the P.R.O. These cover the county courts as well as the P.C.C. itself, but unfortunately they do not include all wills as some estates were too small for death duty.

There is also, on the shelves of the Probate room at the P.R.O., a collection of all the indexes that are in print for the other more local courts in various parts of the country. Some county authorities have done excellent work in printing the indexes that apply to them; others have done little or nothing in this line. But if you find a will that interests you in one of these county indexes you will have to go to that **county record office** to see it or else write for a photocopy. And if you want to search for wills in the counties for which no printed indexes are available you will find that their record offices all have indexes of some sort that you can see there.

Wills used to be in all sorts of strange repositories but on the whole, in recent years, nearly all with the exception of those of the P.C.C. have been sorted out and lodged in their respective county offices. But as the boundaries of dioceses are not the same as those of counties—and both have suffered some changes—the matter is not as simple as it sounds. However the staff of each county record office will at least know where the wills of its own territory should be. For addresses, see Appendix D.

The county of Middlesex and the city of London had more different courts and complications than anywhere else and the wills are now in several repositories. The most likely ones and the places where you can best get further advice are the Guildhall Library in the City and the Greater London Record Office (page 122).

All this sounds complicated—but the point is that thousands of wills from Tudor times onwards (and a few even earlier) do exist and can be found with a bit of persistence and luck. Of course some are disappointing when found. 'All my goods and chattels whatsoever to my true and loving wife' may indicate a devoted husband, but if that is all he has to say you are not much wiser. But some wills tell you a great deal, and things you could never have guessed.

Firstly you nearly always get the status or occupation: knight, gentleman, yeoman, husbandman (a little humbler than the yeoman who was an independent farmer and often richer than a neighbouring gentleman); or again clerk in holy orders or just 'clerk' which meant the same thing, or 'citizen and haberdasher of the City of London'.

Then beyond that you can generally see if the testator is rich or poor which is quite a different matter. The rich man's will is written by a lawyer and peppered with legal expressions such as 'messuages' (houses) and 'hereditaments' (anything you could inherit). The details show the style of living. For instance a fashionable doctor of Hertford in the reign of George II mentions 'my coaches, chaises, chariottes and horses', and again 'my wife's diamonds, and jewels, her gold watch with all the trumpery thereto belonging'. His practice was clearly lucrative.

A poor man's will is more concerned with the means of livelihood—'my plow and plow gere, my two horses, and the corn now standing in Crane-croft Close', and with humbler household fittings, 'my great iron pot—my ten pewter platters'. Beds with all their accessories feature largely, and sheets, hangings and 'coverlids' were important bequests.

Anxiety for the future can often be read between lines penned centuries ago, when social security was non-existent except what neighbours might provide. I am thinking of the will of a husbandman of Great Amwell who as he lay dying bequeathed 'one cowe and one bullock and my daughter Joan' to a cousin in Cheshunt 'and one cowe and one bullock and my sonne John' to a brother in Hertford, 'and the residew of my goods and moveables, and the residew of my children' to his neighbour John Rolfe. And if his relations would not take John and Joan then he prayed that Goodman Rolfe would have them too, 'and the cattle for their upbringing'.

Returning to those in more comfortable circumstances, wills often show their tastes and outlook. I like the Hertfordshire yeoman who (dying in 1557) left to every one of the servants in his house 'one shepe apiece'. These no doubt could be commuted into money when the flock went to market, but we see here a truly pastoral outlook in which sheep were thought of as currency. I found exactly the same thought in another will in the same parish fifty years later: 'To every one of my eight grandchildren one lambe apiece.'

These Hertfordshire wills that I have just quoted were read—not in pursuit of the history of a family but of a house, or rather an estate with cottages as well as a larger house on it. Wills are just as useful for that kind of research as for genealogy, they can transform a name written on an old deed into a human being. One of the owners of this house on which I was working larded his will with classical allusions and mentioned his books on 'Divinitie, Humanitie and Polymathy'. His mind was evidently bent on other subjects than sheep. His son, who became a barrister at Gray's Inn, seemed to think of nothing but music. His will is full of lutes, harpsicords and viols and he left £500 (a large sum in those days) to his lute-maker.

Another way in which wills are extremely useful is in clarifying family relationships. A parish register records only events within the parish, but a will is not limited by local boundaries, but can fill gaps and draw the family together. Parents generally mention all their children, giving the married names of grown-up daughters and often the names of grandchildren.

Don't be surprised if the eldest son gets only a trifling bequest, and jump to the conclusion that there is some unkindness. It may be that the main property has already been settled on him. But even when financial arrangements of this sort had been made in advance it was thought proper for the father to make his last testament on his death bed and leave a souvenir to each child.

Many old wills allude to the failing health of the testator. A very common form of beginning is 'In the name of God. Amen. I —— —— of the parish of ——, yeoman [or gentleman or whatever] being weak and sick in body but of sound mind and memory, thanks be to God, hereby commit my soul to my Maker ——' etc. Such a one is the will of my ancestor, Hanibal Jenkyn, a yeoman farmer of St Keverne in Cornwall who died in 1753. A photostat copy, obtained from the County Record Office in Truro, is now before me. To his eldest son, Athanasius (no: the names are not fictitious) he leaves only 'One guinea in gold to buy a ring to be worn in remembrance of me'; and yet I know that Athanasius was well provided for; perhaps he had married well. To his second son, another Hanibal, he left his 'boats, netts, sayls, and all the materials of fishery whatsoever' including a cellar full of salt in a nearby cove. This reveals a part of his activities of which I had known nothing. His farmhouse with all its stock and furnishings and all the residue of his property is equally divided between his five daughters and their brother, Hanibal, except that his 'dearly beloved wife, Jane, shall have the bed and bedding and all the furniture thereto belonging in the kitchen chamber wherein now I lye'.

This phrase, 'the kitchen chamber', gives us a picture of a typical old-fashioned yeoman's house of this time. I have seen it in many wills and also 'the hall chamber' which meant the same. The front door opened straight into the large room where the family lived, ate, and did much of their cooking. Hanibal's grandfather, whose will I also have (dated 1695) called it 'the hall.' On one side was a small 'parlour', little used I fancy. On the other the principal bedroom with the fourposter. The other bedrooms upstairs under the sloping eaves were of secondary importance.

The practice of leaving a widow her own bed and bedding was very usual. You may see it in hundreds of old wills, including Shakespeare's. It did not imply that she was expected to take her bed and move elsewhere but the very reverse. She was to keep her honoured place in her own home even though it was to become the official property of the next generation. The stipulation about the bed was probably not necessary in a kindly family, but it was conventional to make it so that some mention of the wife, and a loving one, could be included in the will.

That this family was a kindly one whose members were not likely to quarrel is shown by the fact that the father laid down no details of the division of the main property. He trusted his second son to look after his sisters and give them a fair share of the family property when they married. Many wills are full of complicated details about dowries to be paid later and if the estate did not prosper these could become a crippling burden when they fell due.

Don't confine yourself to reading only the wills of your direct ancestors; those of other members of the family can be just as helpful if you are lucky enough to find them. It often happens that a whole bundle of old wills from one family has been preserved together (or all thrown away together). Wills of old grandmothers or childless aunts or uncles can be best of all, for though they do not have much to leave they often make small bequests to nephews and nieces and grandchildren, and throw more light on the family than a rich man who leaves everything to his eldest son.

Hanibal, junior, married his cousin, Elizabeth Incledon, and their daughter of whom I have a portrait in old age (plump and solemn in a frilled cap) was my great-great-grandmother. The Incledons were minor gentry who had settled in St Keverne in the seventeenth century and had ramified into several branches, all very prolific. I was lucky to find twelve of their wills, all eighteenth century, in the Truro Record Office, and when I had read them all I was able to make out a big family tree and also to recognize several of their houses, named in the wills and still standing little changed. They intermarried several times with the Jenkyns and like them drew their incomes from the sea as well as the land. I should never have sorted them out without the wills.

But luck is very variable. These Cornish wills that have helped me so much belong all to my father's mother's family. On his father's side, the Carringtons of Plymouth, I have hardly found a single one. And even if I had found one listed in an index it would have been only a disappointment, for before the last war the archive authorities of Devon collected together all the wills from the local courts in that county to have them conveniently in its record office. In the blitz on Exeter it received a direct hit and all those wills are gone. The only old wills from Devon that remain are those in London that are indexed in the P.C.C. But the catalogue of Devon wills remains to show you what has been lost.

However, most other county record offices have collections of local wills that should give more fortunate results.

5

Parish Registers

Once you are back before the reign of Queen Victoria the chief sources for your family history will be **parish registers**, unless you are among the lucky ones whose forbears possessed the same land for generations and have bundles of old deeds, wills and marriage settlements to prove it. Few of us have this advantage; we may be able to trace some wills, but wills alone—helpful though they are—are not enough. The great advantage of parish registers is that they chronicle the annals of rich and poor alike.

However it would be deceptive to suggest that tracing your family through registers is easy. It is to many people, including me, a delightful and fascinating pursuit, but it can also be frustrating and disappointing. It needs a lot of persistence.

When you have located an ancestor in a particular parish the next step must be to locate its registers. Don't go rushing to the place in question until you have found out where they are and where they can best be seen, for there are several possibilities. They may have been printed in which case you can study them much more easily in one of the big libraries than you could with the originals, but you would miss the charm and character of the old volumes. Only a small fraction of all registers has been printed but that includes most of the central London parishes. Some published lists of registers in print can be found in libraries but many are out of date, and they are being superseded by *The National Index of Parish Registers*, a massive undertaking which is still incomplete though several volumes of it are now available.

The simplest way of finding out whether the registers you want are in print and where you can see either copies or originals is to telephone or write to the appropriate County Record Office (see page 123). It is highly probable that the originals are there, for since the Parochial Records Measure of 1979 the great majority of old registers, together with other historic parish records, have been deposited for safe-keeping in the ideal storage conditions of such offices. There you will have every facility for studying the volumes for as long as you like, generally without charge. There will be expert advice at hand if you need it, and other registers from the same district available too. There will also be such lists and indexes as exist in print, giving particulars of the present whereabouts of registers in other counties.

If the registers you want are still in use at the church, or still being kept there, you must get in touch with the vicar and ask when it will be convenient for you to see them. Most vicars are busy men; many have several churches in their care and may not live near the one in which your interest lies. Don't assume that the registers can be produced at short notice to suit yourself.

Remember that it is the vicar's duty to protect the registers from harm and don't blame him if he won't leave you alone with them. If you inspire enough confidence he may give you a free hand for a reasonable time. Some parsons will hand the matter over to a verger who will spread the volumes out for you on the vestry table and busy himself with some task of his own while you go through them. Or you may have the vicar standing at your elbow, expecting you to look for just one name and be finished in five minutes. This is terrible, for what you want is to follow up any clue you may find. If you discover your ancestor's birth entry it will give you the names of his parents and you will want to turn to another volume to see if their marriage is there. Then you can look for their births, and note any other members of the same family who may appear. But as the fever grows upon you the vicar may be getting restive, and you may feel embarrassment at keeping him waiting.

Then there is the matter of the fee to which he is entitled. For some time past there has been an official rate laid down based on the number of years searched, but this has always been quite impractical and I have never known it enforced. In my experience when the question is raised the vicar generally leaves it to the searcher to give whatever he thinks fit.

Of the dozen or more vicars, previously unknown to me, whom I have approached in this way nearly all have been kind and helpful, but I recall one who stood over me eyeing my every movement so severely that I dared not ask for a second volume. And there was another who flatly refused to allow me or my husband to see any registers at all. We had to wait for his retirement.

When you add to these hazards the fact that vestries are often badly lit and generally cold you will realize that it is a great advantage to be able to see the registers in a record office. On the other hand if you are sure that your family lived in a certain parish you will want to see it for yourself. There may even be a tomb or inscription to their memory in the church or church-yard if you are lucky.

There is still a fourth possibility. In 1597 it was laid down by law that each year the incumbent of each parish must send to the bishop of his diocese a complete copy of the entries in his register for that year. These are known as **Bishops' Transcripts** and were kept mostly in diocesan libraries but many have now been deposited with the county records. Being on loose sheets they are often dogeared, dilapidated and incomplete, but they provide a second chance when part of the original register is missing or difficult of access.

As a last resort you can try to get information by post. If it is just a matter of one item and you have a pretty good idea of when and where it took place you can write either to the record office or the vicar asking for the register to be looked at and the particulars sent if found. The record office staff will answer free of charge as it is part of their regular work, but for the vicar it is an extra chore and you must make it as easy as possible for him. Send a stamped and addressed envelope for reply and a fee (page 123). In neither case can you expect to have a lot done for you. If you want several registers searched over a longish period you must go yourself or employ a professional (page 113).

When at last the registers are set before you, what can you expect from them?

The first thing to hope for is that they will be complete at least for the period you want to cover, and of that there is a fair chance. The keeping of registers was first ordered in 1538 but it was not enforced until the reign of Elizabeth I. Of the thousands of old parishes of England about a quarter have registers starting in 1560 or earlier, and about half date from before 1600. Most of the remainder go back to at least 1700 but many have bad gaps where a volume has been lost. One frequently finds a bad patch during the Pro-tectorate (1649–1660) and some churches lost all their registers through enemy action in the second world war. But by and large the majority have survived.

Under Elizabeth I it was decreed by law that each parish must keep its records in a well-bound book with parchment sheets. This made all the difference, for as long as vicars were noting events on loose pieces of paper their chances of survival were poor. (I said as much about your own notes in Chapter 2.) Books were expensive in the sixteenth century and few if any vicars were so extravagant or far-sighted as to buy three books. So the older volumes contain baptisms, marriages and burials mixed in together. Some vicars put baptisms at the beginning, marriages in the middle, and burials at the end with the book turned upside down, but inevitably one class caught up another and was squeezed into another space until it overran something else. When the necessity of buying a new book was looming large writing tended to get smaller and smaller. Some old registers are beautifully kept and a joy to look at, but some are a terrible muddle.

Today we are all conditioned to filling up forms and treating official documents with care, but some of those early vicars had hardly grasped the object of the exercise. *Buried Margaret, the scolemaster's sister*, wrote a Hertfordshire parson in 1573, and again *Buryed the old man who dwelt on the hethe*. Gradually even he began to grasp that full names were required but for another two centuries and more many registers give deplorably meagre facts.

The bare facts which you can hope to find are: always the date and for baptisms the name of the child and both its parents. For marriages, the full names of both parties and the parishes they belong to. If no parish is mentioned one can assume they are 'of this parish'. For burials one often gets nothing but the name and date. The more conscientious vicars will tell you if the funeral is that of a child and whether a woman is single, married, or a widow, but many of them were idle in this respect, or perhaps they rebelled against the encroachment of bureaucracy. One's heart warms to the vicar who tells one that little bit extra and writes it nicely. But when I read *Buried Richard Lane*, and I can't tell whether it is the old grandfather who has gone, or his son in the prime of life, or the little child whose birth is noted a few lines above, I wish I could take that vicar by the scruff of his neck and shake him.

No one register is the same all the way for each new vicar brings a change of style. Some of the early ones use the formality of Latin, but that presents no great difficulty, as explained on page 93. Many vicars at a rather later time left the keeping of the registers to parish clerks whose spelling might be execrable.

Some indications of social status are generally given but not consistently.

The title of knighthood or of higher rank is always included, and at the opposite end of the social scale illegitimate babies are bluntly specified as 'baseborn', 'bastard', or 'spurious'. But the great majority of parishioners are referred to by their names only, sometimes being short-changed even on that (*Buried old Harding*). Occasionally, however, you will see '*Mr Robert Boon*' or '*Mistress Mary Brook*' being married or buried. This shows that they were much respected people, so much so that the scribe, whether parson or clerk, could not bring himself to write the bare name. And in an original register you may see the names of the more important parishioners written larger and more carefully than the others. The absence of such signs proves nothing for many parsons remembered that all were equal in the sight of God.

Even a baby could be given this sort of respect. In my own local register I see under 1717, *Mr Benjamin Prosser son of Mr Rees Prosser vicar of this parish and of Susannah his wife was born on Tuesday evening ye twentieth day of August and baptised ye twelfth day of September.* You might think it was the clerk showing his humble respect to the parson's child, but it is in Mr Prosser's own hand. He always put more in the register about his own family than about anyone else's. He also used poor-quality ink (people mixed their own at that time) and spluttery pens so that his part of the register is horribly messy. Worst of all, he left the oldest volume lying about in the rectory where Master Benjamin at the age of eleven practised writing his name and various youthful witticisms right across some of the parchment pages that had been exquisitely written more than a century before.

What one hopes for is one of those garrulous vicars who loved to write about his flock. Such a one was Thomas Hassall, vicar of the small village of Great Amwell in Hertfordshire from 1599 to 1657. When any of his parishioners were buried his lively pen went to work telling where they lived, how they died and often giving a frank commentary on their characters.

Elizabeth the wife of Richard Hale of Haly a woman of good repute and in truethe well deserving fell into a burning feaver and so died ——

Edward Shadbolt a labouring man of above three score and ten yeares allwayes a good labourer no spender seildome ate good meate or dranke good drinke or wore good clothes and yet dyed very poore ——

John Allen, a man of good and honest reputation, an old servant to the churche, to guard the chappel doore, to controle unrulye boyes and correct intruding dogges, living poorlye but never miserably ——

Joan Hale an auntient mayde, almost fiftye ——

Phillipe Winckley a notorious owld Bedlam rogue ——

and so on. He often tells us exactly where they are buried, for instance, *Mr John Goodman, a good friend and counsellor and Justice of the Peace —— he lyeth in the chauncell under the comunion table next to owld Hale's wife.* It is amazing how many they packed into the tiny chancel.

It is useless to expect this kind of personal detail except very rarely but even the briefest and dullest register will give occasional touches of the picturesque or of unintended humour. Sample extracts from two mid-seventeenth-century registers are shown in Plates 2 and 3.

A landmark in the keeping of registers was an act brought through Parliament by Lord Hardwick in 1754 to enforce the better recording of marriages. New books were issued to all parishes containing standard forms, (see Plate 1), on which certain details were to be entered: the status of both parties (whether single or previously married), their parishes of residence, the occupation of the bridegroom, and also their signatures, or marks if they couldn't write, and those of two witnesses. This was a real step forward. The signatures make one feel a personal contact with one's ancestors and give some slight idea of status. In the late eighteenth century the majority of the population was still illiterate. A well-written signature shows some education and there is no need to be despondent if there is only a mark, particularly from the bride. Many substantial farmers and tradesmen who could read and write themselves thought this sort of accomplishment unnecessary for their daughters, even undesirable.

Towards the end of the century special books were also issued for recording baptisms and burials and the amount of information becomes a little fuller, but some vicars and their clerks remained incorrigibly slipshod about filling them up. So we come into the nineteenth century where registers were on the whole properly kept.

In searching a register experience helps and some advice may be of use.

It often happens that you have to work against time. You may have come a long way to the church or record office and have to return that evening. If you fail to find what you want where you expected it there is generally something else that can be tried. If you have success one thing leads to another and the time available is often too short. Don't waste it in the early stages.

The first thing is to be well-prepared beforehand with an exact list of what you are going to look for, including careful calculations of the most likely dates for each item. You should also have ready the *possible* dates which will cover a longer period than the *likely* ones. As you go you will of course note down any other occurrences of the surname, for though you may fail to find the particular person you are looking for you may see other members of his family and perhaps a couple who could turn out to be his parents.

Be methodical. Search carefully. It is the easiest thing in the world after a page or two to let your eyes go wandering down the page too fast with an occasional skid over a faint or difficult bit of writing. It is maddening at the end of the day to start wondering if you have missed the item you wanted most. You may be safe from this danger when dealing with the later registers where the surname comes in the same position in each entry, but in the older volumes where all sorts of items are mixed together, some being of one line and some of two or more, the surname may come anywhere. Make sure you see it for each entry. A piece of paper held below the line and moved down as you read can help you to avoid skipping.

Of course a moment may come when you see that you won't have time to finish the desired period of years and you may not have another chance of seeing this register again for months. Then you face the choice: 'Shall I do a few more years properly and leave the rest, or shall I go into top gear and skim the longer period at speed?' You may well decide on the latter and be glad you did, for the name may catch your eye in the last few minutes. But in any case make it clear in your notes what you have done: so many years (exact dates) 'searched', and so many (dates again) 'skimmed'. That latter part may be worth going over again some day.

For of course you are keeping notes of what is done. In the excitement of the chase it is easy to forget the routine but you will pay for it later. In that delightful moment when a pile of registers is placed before you, your note-book should be open beside you with the name of the parish written as a heading. As soon as you have decided where to begin write the particulars of your starting place—*Baptisms 1760*—or whatever it is, and when you stop fill in that date too, and then further details of any other patches you may search. You may sadly have nothing at all to enter under these hopeful headings, except that a certain name did not appear, but even that is useful as elimination. I have searched dozens of registers in Devon for my father's ancestors of the name of Carrington and my notebooks have pages of head-ings and dates followed by the brief statement *No Cs*, (Carringtons being very rare in the south-west before 1750) but at least I knew exactly what ground had been covered and at last I did find the baptism I wanted.

The registers of a big town present a very different problem from those of a village. In the village the full human statistics of one year may occupy less than a page and a whole century can be searched inside an hour. In a town there may be several parishes, each one dealing in large numbers. In Plymouth where my Carrington ancestors lived in the eighteenth century the register of St Andrew's alone often contained over seven hundred births in one year, a high proportion of them illegitimate, owing to the large number of sailors who came ashore. The deaths also were abnormally high in relation to the permanent population because so many of the babies died. I spent many days in the Exeter Record Office going through the various registers and marking up my stint each day. In the end it was in St Charles's parish that I found my great-great-grandfather's christening. His parents' marriage was there too just a year earlier but his own marriage was in Stoke Damerel, now swallowed up in Devonport.

It often happens that in spite of good evidence connecting someone with a certain town, yet in reality he lived on its outskirts which might be part of a neighbouring parish. So if you are sure your ancestor lived in some town and yet can't find him in its registers the best course is to study a detailed map and cast about among the nearest surrounding villages. You can also visit churchyards and read tombstones but not many are legible from much before 1800. Inscriptions inside churches are much better preserved, but they represent only a tiny fraction of those who have died in the village. The registers with all their faults are far more comprehensive.

Keep in mind that church records give—not births and deaths—but baptisms and burials. As regards date this makes little difference, for babies were normally baptised as soon as possible owing to the high risk of their dying and a strong faith in the importance of the rite; nor could burial be long delayed. But it does sometimes account for the difficulty in finding a record which you thought you could place for certain. For a baby though born in one parish could be taken to another to be baptised because of some family connection, and again a man who died in one place could be buried elsewhere to gratify a private wish. I think of my own great-grandfather who died in Bath, murmuring, 'Don't bury me among the pavements and lamp-posts.' His son chose a churchyard on a beautiful hillside some miles outside the city. But precious new-born babies were not taken far for baptism, nor, unless the family was very rich, were the dead transported far before the days of railways. So if the trail suddenly fails cast about nearby.

I have perhaps stressed the difficulties more than the pleasures of register-hunting, but it is best to know the worst of the pitfalls before you start. And if you are disappointed in finding the particular thing you want don't immediately give up. If you have the time, browse through the register keeping a sharp look out for any trace of the family at any date, and even if you still don't see them you will at least get something of the flavour of a past time and perhaps an unexpected laugh.

Searching parish registers has been transformed in recent years by the Mormons (the Church of Jesus Christ of Latter-Day Saints) who are encouraged to trace and baptise their ancestors. Their huge collection of microfilmed records includes over 32,000,000 British entries of baptisms and marriages, but no burials. Its index is known as the **C.F.I.** (Computer File Index) or **I.G.I.** (International Genealogical Index). Microfiches of it, arranged by county, can be searched at the Society of Genealogists (pages 64, 122) or at Mormon branch libraries. Many County Record Offices also hold their own parts of the Index.

Within each county the entries are indexed by surname so that you can very quickly find the one you want, or if it is at all common, only too many. Date, parish and parents' names will help you to identify a baptism, but don't assume it is yours without proper connecting links.

The C.F.I. is far from complete and suffers from human error. Ideally its entries should be checked against the original registers. But it does bring together items from far more registers than you would ever be able to search individually.

In earlier times, faith was strong, and Christian baptism and burial were almost universal. During most of the period on which you are likely to be working, the great majority of the population fortunately belonged to the established church. However, after the Reformation the Roman Catholics maintained separate services as far as possible, and in the next century the Quakers and other Puritan sects began to go their own way regardless of persecution. In the 18th century, the Methodist movement greatly increased the numbers of Nonconformists, but until 1806, when the law was altered, many of them married in the local Anglican church to ensure the ceremony was legal. The whole picture is dealt with in Vol. 2 (Nonconformist churches) and Vol. 3 (R.C. and Jewish records) of the *National Index of Parish Registers* (see page 119).

The largest collection of **non-parochial registers** (that is, non-Anglican) is at the P.R.O. in Chancery Lane. It has registers of some churches of foreigners in England, and some Jewish records, and it also holds Recusant Rolls giving lists of Catholics during the time when they suffered many disabilities.

For **Quaker records**, which are better preserved than those of other dissenters, enquire at Friends House, London (page 135).

6

Other Parish Records

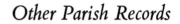

The importance of parish registers in the hunt for family history is well-known but it is little recognized that there are a lot more parish records that may be helpful.

Before the mid-nineteenth century when the general movement towards the centralization of government began to gather momentum, every parish controlled its own affairs to a remarkable degree. Through its vestry meetings it levied its own local taxes, looked after its own sick and poor, maintained its own roads and was—up to a point—responsible for its own law and order.

All this work left behind it a mass of miscellaneous records, kept often in an amateurish and naïve style. Much of it has perished at the hands of well-intentioned persons who from time to time have waged war on dust and cobwebs in old church vestries and on anything that they might class as rubbish. But also a fair amount has survived and is now better valued. For the most part it has been handed over to the local record office where it is tenderly cared for and available to anyone who would like to see it; but some of it still remains in parish chests in the vestries where it originated.

So when you go to see parish registers don't forget to ask whether there are any other parish records available—Rate Books, Vestry Books, Churchwardens' Accounts, or the like. Any of these may survive from the early eighteenth century. But their survival varies greatly from one parish to another; there may be nothing or anything, and the name written on the cover of the book or series of books varies too and may be different again from those just mentioned. But accept anything and at least have a look.

To appreciate what you may find requires a little understanding of how parishes were run, but a very little will do. The Vestry meetings consisted of regular gatherings of the leading residents (elected for the purpose) and held officially in the vestry, but in fact often adjourning to the local inn where a flow of liquid refreshment helped the proceedings along. **Vestry Books** contain minutes of these discussions and can mention all sorts of topics often giving personal sidelights on individuals, such as '*It is resolved that if the pew lately errected by Mr John Pallett be not speedily reduced in height and that at his own expense it will be totally removed by parish*'. Everyone present signed his name (in the Vestry Books I have seen) and the signatures or marks of the illiterate can be most revealing.

But the subject that took up most of the Vestry's time was the care of the poor of the parish. Their method was to elect two overseers for the year from among their number to be in charge of all arrangements, and to levy a rate on all householders to provide the necessary money. (They managed on wonderfully little compared with the Welfare State.) The details of their expenditure were chronicled either in the Vestry Book or in a special **Poor Book**, or perhaps in a book headed **Overseers' Accounts**. Such books often contain minute details of small sums spent on purchases for the parish poor: '*2 shifts for the widow Heady, 6s 8d: a petticoat for Betty Boiling, 6s: a pair of shoes for each of Dick Rabbet's children, 12s.*' (See also Plate 4.)

You may feel sure that your ancestors were not in this class at the receiving end of village charity, but the accounts of what has been done can often involve the more affluent parishioners and mention them by name. To start with you will get the names of the overseers who were chosen as being respectable persons whom everyone trusted. But more important than that— there should be a list, compiled at the beginning of each year, of all the householders with the amount they had to pay graded in accordance with the property they owned or rented. It is nearly always headed by the squire or principal landowner, followed by the more prosperous farmers, inn-keepers or tradesmen, and tailing off to mere cottagers who paid each a few pence if they were self-supporting.

These lists can be most useful in supplementing what you have found in the register. For—it must be faced—a register can leave you feeling starved of facts. A family can live a long time in a parish and perhaps play an active part in it without any one of its members being born or dying, and marriage can often take place elsewhere. But these **Rate Lists**, as they are generally called, show the whole community in residence. You may have thought you had lost your family, but there they are—or not—paying their rates, and perhaps taking their turn in local administration. Their place in the list and the amount they pay will give some idea of their property, and you may also get a hint as to its nature, or the actual name of a farm: '*Mr Sprackling for the Manor Farm 6" 8, ditto for his own land 4" 6, Mr Friend for Sweetapples 5" 6, Mr King for the forge 2" 6, ditto for his dwelling house,*' and so on.

Churchwardens' Accounts refer mainly to expenditure incurred for the church, payments to carpenters, stone masons, bell-ringers, and other assistants, but they too have plenty of human interest and often include a similar list of parishioners—or rather heads of households—with the contribution expected from them. There might be a special appeal for coping with some natural calamity or an unexpected expense, and then it is gratifying to see one of one's own forbears behaving handsomely—if he does.

Another set of records giving lists of landowners arranged in parishes is that of the **Land Tax assessments**. This was a nationwide tax, concerned largely with establishing the right to vote, and is set out in a much more professional style than the local efforts just mentioned. But it was organized by parishes and is useful in the same kind of way as the local rate lists. The chief difference is that it lists owners rather than residents, and owners could live elsewhere. However after 1786 occupiers of houses are given as well as owners. These lists if they exist are now mostly in county record offices.

One important record that nearly every parish does possess is a visual one —a very detailed map of approximately 1840. They are called the Tithe Apportionment Maps, **Tithe Maps** for short, and were made when the old system of paying the vicar in tithes of farm produce was changed for the more practical one of fixed rents. For this purpose each parish was minutely surveyed, every wood and field, garden and building shown and numbered, and an accompanying swag of sheets gave particulars for each number, its nature, its owner and its occupier. Nothing so ambitious of this sort had been attempted since Domesday Book. Three copies were made of each map and there should be one in the church, one at the County Record Office and one at the Tithe Redemption Commission Office in London.

If you think you know where your family was living at about this date you may find it intriguing to study one of these maps and possibly identify the house they lived in. Of course it may have been pulled down long ago and the whole district rebuilt, but in spite of so many changes England is still rich in old streets, old villages, old houses. The house may still be standing. And there may be other things you can learn from the map.

Nowadays many people especially in large towns hardly know what parish they are in and local government has become such a complicated affair that the parish council is overshadowed by other authorities; but in the study of old records it is very necessary to be parochially minded.

On the whole, in country regions, parishes coincide fairly obviously with villages and small towns, but for an outlying farm or isolated house the matter may be doubtful and in checking don't be satisfied with finding out what parish it is in now, for there has been much adjustment of boundaries in the last century and a half. On the edges of large towns and in areas of much modern growth, the whole arrangement may have been altered. But from the Middle Ages to the accession of Queen Victoria there was hardly any change in such matters.

If in doubt about parish boundaries the best place to look is in the appropriate **County History** which you will find in any good reference library in that region. Every county has at least one history, many of them handsome illustrated books composed by antiquarians of the 18th or early 19th centuries. They are inclined to treat their subject by parishes, recording the known annals of each one in turn, and nearly all have maps showing the parish boundaries from which you can check those that concern yourself.

In old country histories and in most old documents parishes are listed in groups called *Hundreds*. These were county subdivisions that dated from pre-Conquest times. Their ancient names are for the most part forgotten and unused today, but if you are searching old records for a particular parish it will help you to know the name of the hundred to which it belonged.

As we have seen, most of the regular taxation was organized locally up to about 1800 but from time to time a nationwide tax was laid on the whole country and collected by parishes. One that is of special interest to researchers is the **Hearth Tax** which was levied between 1662 and 1668. Householders were required to pay so much according to the size of their houses, and the unit of measurement was the number of hearths or fireplaces it contained.

What makes the returns from this tax especially valuable is that they are preserved in such detail (unlike the later windows tax for instance). Like some of the parochial records mentioned earlier in this chapter, they give complete lists of householders in each village, showing residents rather than absent owners. But whereas the survival of vestry books, rate books and the like is a very chancy matter and it is exceptional to have them before the mid-eighteenth century, the Hearth Tax returns from a full century earlier are almost complete. They consist of parchment rolls and are kept at the Public Record Office where you may see them if you have a reader's ticket (page 27). This involves some trouble and because of their age they may be a little difficult to read. But if you are really keen to catch a glimpse of the town or village where you think your forbears were living in the reign of Charles

II it is something you can do. But make sure you know the name of the hundred before you start, as that will make it much easier to find.

For some English counties the Hearth Tax has been printed and you can have this glimpse into the past with no trouble at all in the county reference library. As the books are indexed you have the added advantage that if you fail to find the surname you want in the parish where you expect it, you can look easily to see if it occurs elsewhere in the county, instead of spending a long time peering at the lists of a few nearby villages on the original rolls.

Under the heading of each village name you will have a list of the heads of households, with the number of hearths beside each. This gives a good idea of the size of the houses. Everyone however poor had at least one hearth but the very poorest, those on parish charity, were exempt. At that time the building of many separate rooms with proper fireplaces and chimneys was still a modern innovation except for the very rich. In these lists the majority of the householders have one, two or three hearths. Four or five might indicate a substantial yeoman's farmhouse, roomy but with few modern improvements. Nine or ten signifies a fine house, probably that of a gentleman, but there are many possible variations between old and new, rich and poor. At the upper end of the scale Hatfield House, built in 1611, by Elizabeth's minister Robert Cecil, had ninety-seven.

An even more comprehensive set of personal names may be found in the Protestation Rolls of 1641. At that date all adult males were required to take an oath of allegiance to the Crown and the Protestant religion, and in many cases the names of 'refusers' were also given. Until recently these rolls were rather inaccessible but now a number of counties have had their own sections printed or photocopied so that copies may be seen in their record offices. The rolls give names only but, being arranged by parishes and also indexed, they can be very useful for locating families.

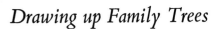

7

Drawing up Family Trees

Making family trees can be very enjoyable. You are setting out the results of your researches in an orderly, visual way and may feel the pleasure that any collector feels when displaying his specimens to good advantage.

The exact way of doing it depends on your special object. If you want to show all your known relations, alive or dead, you will need a wide sheet of paper to accommodate families of cousins across the page, but also enough depth to show the forbears who connect you together. Try it out in rough several times until you see how best to fit it in.

If families are large it may be impossible to keep all of each generation on one line. In many printed pedigrees where space is limited connecting lines may take you down the page and the children of one brother be far below those of another, but it is much more satisfactory to see them on a level. In any case the line of descent should come directly from the sign of the parents' marriage (=). It can then turn horizontally right or left or both ways connecting all the children of the marriage.

Or perhaps you want to show your direct ancestry only, or to draw a tree which will illustrate the relationship between two particular families (like the one on page 55), or to concentrate on one line which takes you back to a particular ancestor (as in the one on page 81). This tree is very simple because its aim is merely to show the link between Edward III, at the top, and Margaret Warner, at the bottom, side-stepping into the female line where necessary. The only names given in each generation are the name of the direct ancestor through whom the line passes and, if this is a woman, of her husband.

Don't clutter your tree with too many facts. It is not meant to take the place of your notebooks, but rather to give a general view, showing relationships and only the key facts. Repeat surnames frequently so that all is clear at a glance. Some of these points are illustrated on the next few pages with examples taken from my own family. I have used them because fictitious pedigrees would be useless, and there is no other real family with which I would take such liberties.

Overleaf is a pedigree showing the descendants of my father's great-great-grandfather in the male line. It ends with my own generation for which I give no details beyond our names and dates and an indication as to whether or not the line continues.

I begin with Joseph because he is the first of our Carrington forbears that we know for certain. We have a probable origin for him (going a good way back) but the essential link remains unproved.

The choice of what facts to include is not easy, but the further back one goes the more it is limited by one's knowledge. For instance, I give the full details of the marriage of Joseph and Barbary because it is nearly all that I know of them, and Barbary's second marriage is significant as giving a date by which Joseph was dead, and a link with the grandchild who was named after her second husband. After this I am limited here by space and have omitted some details that might well be included, such as the names of children who died young. And on a larger page I should have moved my own family more to the right so that my cousin Edmund could have been in line with us instead of being squeezed in above.

An overall pattern emerges. After Joseph, two successive only sons (or so it seems), then three large families with five sons in each, and yet dwindling again in the male line. It may be that my great-uncles Robert and Arthur who vanished overseas in the 1840s left descendants abroad, otherwise the only continuing Carringtons from all those shown here are the one family in New Zealand, which is, I am glad to say, flourishing.

As both I and my father were the youngest of large families the generations are unusually long, so that only two steps, from me to my grandfather, take us into the reign of George III, and my grandfather actually saw Napoleon when he was brought into Plymouth aboard the *Bellerophon* in 1815.

Joseph Carrington = Barbary Morrish =
                            m.1747 Plymouth
                                (St Charles)

Henry Carrington = Rosamund Verant
1748 - 1808 Tradesman m. 1775 Stoke Damerel
of Plymouth Dock

Nicholas Toms Carrington = Anne - - -
1777 - 1830 . Schoolmaster 1786 - 1840
and poet . Bur. Coombe Hay
near Bath . M.I. (D.N.B.)

Henry Edmund Carrington	Elizabeth	Rosamund
1806-59 „ Editor "Bath	b. 1808	b.1810
Chronicle" . M.I. Bath Abbey		
= Emily Heywood Johns		
(See Tree 2)		

Henry	Emily	George	Lucy	Alexander Randal
1840 -	1842 -	1843 -	1846-	1848 - 1920
1920	1920	1903	1929	Fruit farmer N.Z.
Clergyman		Journalist	=C.Hugon	= Anne Marsack

1 da.

Hubert   2 da.
Carrington
         d.1940

3 sons in N.Z.

Philip	Christopher	Arthur Hugh
1892-1975	1893-1916	1895-1947

(2) Nicholas Toms, Attorney of Plymouth Dock
m. 1761 Plymouth (St Andrews)

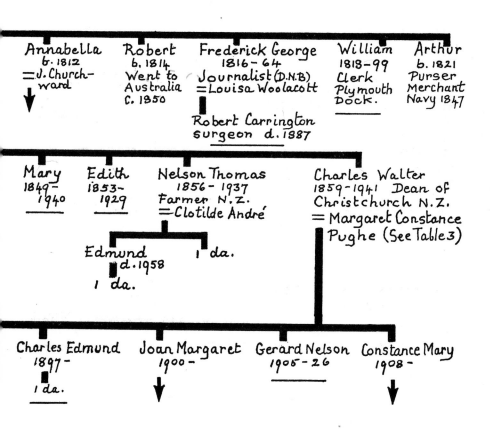

Annabella
b. 1812
= J. Church-
ward

Robert
b. 1814
Went to
Australia
c. 1850

Frederick George
1816 - 64
Journalist (D.N.B)
= Louisa Woolacott

William
1818 - 99
Clerk
Plymouth
Dock.

Arthur
b. 1821
Purser
Merchant
Navy 1847

Robert Carrington
surgeon d. 1887

Mary
1849 -
1940

Edith
1853 -
1929

Nelson Thomas
1856 - 1937
Farmer N.Z.
= Clotilde André

Charles Walter
1859 - 1941 Dean of
Christchurch N.Z.
= Margaret Constance
Pughe (See Table 3)

Edmund
d. 1958
1 da.

1 da.

Charles Edmund
1897 -
1 da.

Joan Margaret
1900 -

Gerard Nelson
1905 - 26

Constance Mary
1908 -

The tree on the opposite page illustrates my paternal grandmother's descent from the Incledons of St Keverne, Cornwall. It differs from the last one in that its chief purpose is to show the relationship between her parents (fourth cousins) and how she was descended three times over from the couple at the top. This intermarrying of neighbouring families in country districts was very common in days when a journey far from home was a rarity and choice limited.

In this case I have given only those through whom the direct descent comes and none of their many brothers and sisters. My chief sources for the earlier generations are the St Keverne registers and a number of wills. It is from these that I take the descriptions 'gentleman' and 'yeoman', but in fact I don't think there was much to choose between the Incledons and Jenkyns who were both moderately comfortable with their farms and fishing boats. Some information as to status or occupation adds interest to family trees, especially when it is definite, but it is often difficult to express briefly. I can't say exactly what Bennet John did or was, but soon after his marriage he moved to Plymouth where he later set up his eldest son as a banker. The bank eventually failed and Henry fell back on his artistic talent to support his family, having previously gone back to Cornwall to marry his cousin Maria.

Incidentally it was after the move to Plymouth that the family began to write their surname in the English manner with a final 's'. John is the Cornish form. Such changes were not unusual at this date and earlier.

The layout of this kind of tree so as to bring prospective spouses together can generally be contrived with a little care.

A quite different way of setting out your ancestry is the tabular form

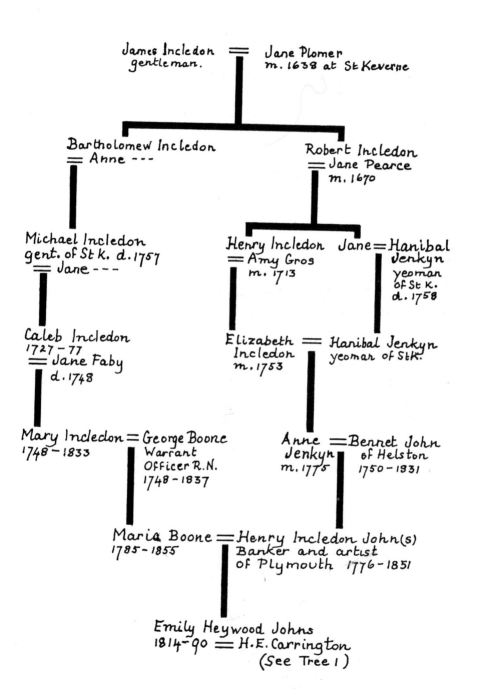

James Incledon gentleman. = Jane Plomer m. 1638 at St Keverne

Bartholomew Incledon = Anne ---

Robert Incledon = Jane Pearce m. 1670

Michael Incledon gent. of St K. d. 1757 = Jane ---

Henry Incledon = Amy Gros m. 1713

Jane = Hanibal Jenkyn yeoman of St K. d. 1758

Caleb Incledon 1727-77 = Jane Faby d. 1748

Elizabeth Incledon m. 1753 = Hanibal Jenkyn yeoman of St K.

Mary Incledon 1748-1833 = George Boone Warrant Officer R.N. 1748-1837

Anne Jenkyn m. 1775 = Bennet John of Helston 1750-1831

Maria Boone 1785-1855 = Henry Incledon John(s) Banker and artist of Plymouth 1776-1851

Emily Heywood Johns 1814-90 = H.E. Carrington (See Tree 1)

I	II	III	IV
¹ The Very Rev Charles Walter Carrington MA b. Bath 1859 d. Limpley Stoke, near Bath, 1941	¹ Henry Edmund Carrington 1806-59	¹ Nicholas Toms Carrington 1777 - 1830	¹ Henry Carrington
			² Rosamund Verant
		² Anne – 1786 -1840	³
			⁴
	² Emily Heywood Johns 1814-90	³ Henry Incledon John(s) 1776 - 1852	⁵ Bennet John
			⁶ Anne Jenkyn
		⁴ Maria Boone 1785 - 1855	⁷ George Boone
			⁸ Mary Incledon
² Margaret Constance Pughe b. Bangor, Wales, 1862 d. Bath 1930	³ The Rev Evan Pughe BA 1806 - 69	⁵ The Rev. Evan Pugh(e) d. 1830	⁹ Humphrey Pugh
			¹⁰ Elizabeth Lewis
		⁶ Anne Owen 1783 -1869	¹¹
			¹²
	⁴ Margaret Parry 1827-74	⁷ Robert Parry d. before 1840	¹³ Robert Parry
			¹⁴
		⁸ Margaret Warner 1806 - 1883	¹⁵ William Warner
			¹⁶ Elizabeth Heveningham

shown above. This is for direct ancestors only, and has the advantage of being neat and compact. By using Roman numerals for the generations and arabic for the individuals in each column and by placing them always in regular order—husband above, wife below—you have a handy form of reference which you can use in your notes if so minded. This is a standard method and most genealogists would know that IV 6 can only be your father's mother's father's mother.

Of course you will need it much bigger than this to give yourself room for more details and more generations.

Another way to show direct ancestry is in a circle with yourself in the middle. It is really the same method as the one just described but opened up like a fan so as to get more room out on the perimeter. It is fun doing it if you enjoy patterns, but a bit discouraging if you don't know a good many ancestors as the blank segments keep getting larger with all the rest, and you are terribly conscious of the gaps.

Just to make a change I am putting my husband's forbears in this example. But on this small scale there is no room for details.

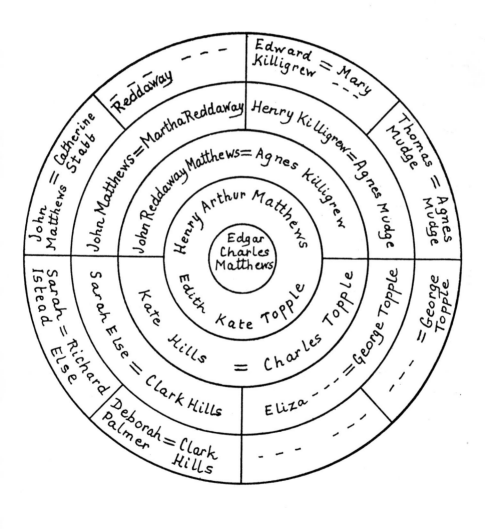

8

Help from Libraries

From the start of your researches you will naturally make full use of libraries. The amount of help available will depend on where the library is—or rather where you are and which one you can conveniently go to. For when it comes to the kind of detailed collections of facts needed for genealogy each big library specializes in its own locality, and for the best results you should visit the chief reference library of the county where you think your ancestors lived.

However we can't all go where we like all the time, and in the meantime you can see what the chief reference library of your own district has to offer. It is sure to have a genealogical section and that will include a number of books that will at least give you ideas to follow up later.

There may for instance be *A Genealogical Guide* by J. B. Whitmore, or *The Genealogists' Guide* by G. Marshall. Each of these lists in alphabetical order families for which pedigrees of three or more generations exist in print and tells you where to find them. Genealogists have been working for centuries on family histories and if one of them has done some of your work for you, you may as well take advantage of it. Don't be discouraged if the name you are looking for isn't there, or too hopeful if it is. The guides won't tell you anything about the family except where to find information about it, perhaps in a standard reference book such as Burke's *Landed Gentry* (but it will be an old edition), or a *County History*, or a *Visitation Book* (see page 78), or a journal of a learned society. You will probably have to ask the librarian how to find it, and it may be that you will have to wait until you can visit a bigger library. If and when you do track down the pedigree you may find that it was compiled two or three centuries ago and has no apparent link with your own family. Even so if the name is at all uncommon copy down the chief points and exactly where to find it again, for a connection may one day appear.

In fact if your name is unusual it is well worth looking in any of the general reference books that give lists of names from a wide field in earlier times. Provided they are alphabetical or well indexed it can be quickly and easily done, and if you note all the occurrences of the name with dates and localities—say before 1800—you can gradually build up a picture showing the chief concentrations of the name in earlier times.

It is not much use doing this with modern reference books such as telephone directories as people have moved about so much in the last century, and also multiplied so greatly. In 1800 the population of Great Britain was less than a fifth of what it is now, and far more families were still living where their forbears had lived, so there is much more point in locating bearers of your surname then or earlier. But don't assume they are all your ancestors. Even if all the bearers of one rare name are descended from one fourteenth-century ancestor, they could have split into several distinct branches by 1500. Just note them hopefully for future reference. It is a good idea to have one notebook where you have them all set out in their local groups, hoping that one day you will link on to one of them. But if your surname is a regular one that might arise independently in many districts you can't play the game this way at all.

But when you can visit the chief library in your ancestor's home county you will find a great deal more that applies directly to your problem. It will have, to start with, all its own county histories and smaller histories of individual towns and parishes. Old guide-books too can be fascinating to look through when you have a personal interest in the locality and often contain a great many names of prominent members of the community, such as town councillors and those in charge of churches, schools, and the principal inns and other places of business. There should also be old directories of the neighbourhood. These began to appear for most districts from about 1800. Very old copies are somewhat rare and precious but most of the big libraries have a few of their own district. These can be of the greatest value to you in pinning down your family at a fairly exact address at a given date. But unfortunately the earliest directories were far from comprehensive. If the person you are looking for is not listed as a resident, don't assume he wasn't there.

Another means of locating individuals is by **Poll Books**. These are the lists of men entitled to vote in general elections when suffrage was strictly limited by the ownership of property. They are arranged by the parishes where the property was, and show the more prosperous inhabitants of the county, but these include many farmers and tradesmen, as well as the gentry.

The variation between counties in the way they have made their old records available to the public is very great. Some have edited and printed a great many things of this sort, including for instance the proceedings of the Quarter Sessions (enthralling reading whether or not you find any ancestors), indexes of local wills, catalogues of marriage licences, hearth tax returns (page 49), manorial documents (page 85) and so on. You must simply see what there is in the principal library of the region where your search lies and try anything that looks promising. And don't assume that what you see on the shelves is all there is. Most big libraries have more books in reserve which can be produced if asked for, and some of them now have microfilm of old records which apply to the county (as for instance the relevant parts of the Victorian census returns) of which the originals are in London. So ask the librarian if any of these things are available.

Some parish registers have been printed and big libraries should certainly have those of their own region. If they include the parish you are specially concerned with you are extraordinarily lucky—make the most of it—and if you see any printed registers for parishes anywhere near the one you want, try them too. Although it is true that in earlier times people spent more of their lives in one place than we do, they weren't rooted to one spot. They married in neighbouring parishes and might move to a new home a few miles away. The higher the social status, the more mobile they were. Printed registers with indexes are so easy to check for names in a few minutes if you have them to hand—compared with the originals where you may toil for hours and achieve less—that if you see some on the shelf for anywhere near the parish you want you should have a look. The motto of the genealogist must always be—Try everything.

Some large cities have particularly notable borough libraries with fine collections of material for local history and genealogy; apart from these you will do best at the **county reference library**. This should not be confused with the **county record office** (page 32) whose chief concern is with original documents. However, there may be some overlapping between these two, but fortunately they are generally housed close together in the building complex of the County Hall, and neither of them involves any ticket or payment.

If you are within easy reach of London you have the advantage of using the best possible libraries, chief among them the **British Museum Library**. It has lately been decreed that this great institution shall henceforth be called the **British Library** and the new title is now being used officially. But as its old name is familiar to millions throughout the world and its initials, B.M., are used in the notes and references of thousands of existing books, while the new one as yet conveys little to most people, I shall continue to use the old name or its initials for the sake of clarity.

Unfortunately this unparalleled collection of printed works is suffering other troubles besides a change of name, for it has outgrown its premises, imposing though they are, and is under threat of total removal. But since some years must elapse before the great upheaval takes place, it is probably still useful to describe it as it is.

Its great merit is that it has everything that is in print, almost everything that ever was printed in Britain, and a vast amount from other countries too. Here you can read all the family histories that have been printed, all the registers of schools and colleges and professional bodies for as far back as they go, all the local histories down to humble village guide-books without having to go to that locality to find them, all the journals of learned societies to which you may have been given references in the *Guide to Genealogy*, the Heralds' Visitations, the earliest editions of reference books, any published book you can name. The vast circular room itself is something of an inspiration; the space (but alas not enough), the dignity, the portentous hush, and all those leather-backed books and leather-topped tables. I never go into it without a sense of euphoria. But I must admit this can change to frustration. There are snags.

The first is that you must have a Reader's Ticket, as for the P.R.O., and the same one won't do. Get your application form in good time in case there is any delay. It must be signed by an official person who can vouch for your character. You must establish that you need the ticket for serious research. If you come to the Museum unprepared they may be willing to give you a short-term ticket but this wastes time and it is much better to have a proper one. Otherwise admission is free.

The second snag is the lack of space already mentioned. It is especially bad during the summer when scholars and searchers are drawn here from all over the world. If you are not here soon after opening time (page 122) you may not get a seat, and without a seat you can't order a book. So when you make your entry don't stand gazing about you awestruck (as well you might) or linger at the enquiry desk to ask questions (you can do that later) but press forward with the single-mindedness of an old hand at Musical Chairs. The books most useful to genealogy are to the left of the entrance, the numbers above the shelves ranging from 2098 to 2101. So turn left briskly, find a vacant place as near to this region as you can, reserve it by putting some of your possessions on the table, and only then can you relax. Note the number of your seat before you stray away from your base, for you can easily lose your bearings and wander round and round, like a small gnat lost in the dome of St Paul's.

The next snag is that when you order a book it probably won't arrive (they are brought to your seat) for at least an hour, so get some orders in as quickly as possible. This is done by finding what you want in the catalogue and filling in its particulars on one of the order forms provided, being especially careful to copy the shelf-number correctly. You then post this in a box at the centre desk. If the shelf-number given in the catalogue is between 2000 and 2119b the book is on one of the public shelves and you can find it for yourself. It is most irritating to wait over an hour to be told that you could have helped yourself to the book all the time.

The catalogue is formidable. It consists of over two thousand large volumes arranged as a circular maze in the centre of the room. Books are indexed chiefly by authors, so it is important to be well prepared not only with authors' surnames but their Christian names too or at least initials. If you are so prepared it is easy to find a book under its author's name however obscure it may be. So far so good. But a great many books you might want for genealogical purposes, such as registers of various sorts, have no authors, only editors or compilers whose names you would hardly know, or they may be issued by some learned body such as the British Record Society or the Index Society, but how are you to know? This difficulty of finding things in the catalogue is to my mind the worst of the snags, and after using it over a period of twenty years I can still walk round and round it trying this and that while my euphoria turns into frustration. But here are a few points.

Family histories, if they exist in print, are listed under the surnames of the families, and it is worth just looking to see if there is anything about the one in which you are interested. At the same time you can see if any past member of the family ever published anything. You never know; one of your great-uncles may have written his memoirs and no one ever mentioned it again.

Directories—local and professional—are all together under D. Magazines and journals are all grouped under P as 'Periodical Publications'. They fill many volumes and are subdivided under the cities in which they are published—one of those minor snags which catch you when you think you are nearly there; but most of the journals you are likely to want are published in London. Army and Navy records and those of some other national institutions come under 'England' (you might never have thought of that).

All the parish registers that have been printed must be there but they are not easy to find unless you want one of the London parishes which are all on the open shelves. On a small set of shelves at the inner end of table O, near the centre, are a few important books to aid genealogy, including some paper-backed handlists showing the dates of all existing registers which are printed and which may be found in the leading genealogical libraries. Recent publications on this subject are also placed here.

Histories and guide-books of towns and parishes can generally be found under the name of the town in question and sometimes their registers too (but this is not to be relied on). County Histories are on the open shelves; and it is a good idea to look up the county name in the catalogue as there may be a county Records Society that has published local records.

As well as the main catalogue there is a subject index, but this was made in 1900, with supplements added every five years. After trying that the main catalogue seems simple. You can of course take your problems to the enquiry desk and the staff there will advise you to the best of their ability, but even they don't know all the answers.

When you have put in your orders for the books you have found in the catalogue and decided to abandon the search for others that have proved too elusive, then you can settle down to enjoy the very large number of splendid reference books that are on the shelves. Besides the section marked *Genealogy* those headed *Topography, Biography, Encyclopedias* and *Periodicals* are full of good things, and as you take down one book after another the euphoria begins to return.

Among the periodicals *The Gentleman's Magazine* is especially recommended. Starting in 1731, it continued for well over a century giving not only news and comment on innumerable subjects but a social section at the end of each monthly number made up of marriages, deaths, appointments and promotions for a large part of the population. Of course it is chiefly concerned with the upper classes but is very much less exclusive than you might expect. It is bound in annual volumes each of which has an index of persons, and together they occupy a large and tempting block on the shelves. Too tempting in my case sometimes. I start by looking for a particular name, and am led astray to enjoy the period flavour of the volume, and to take down others when I ought to be grappling with the catalogue.

There is in fact no lack of material to pass the time usefully while waiting for books, it is only the time that is never enough. But it should be explained that once you have noted the shelf-marks of the books you want, you can order them for the next day or several days ahead, and have them available as soon as you arrive. You can also write or even telephone to order books in advance of some future visit.

The other public library in London that offers outstanding help to the genealogist is the **Guildhall Library**. Compared with the B.M. it is a haven of rest because the snags that beset you in the bigger library are all missing. It is true that it is much less comprehensive in its scope, but in the realm of English history, topography, and the sort of social and personal records that the genealogist thrives on, it is excellent. For records of London it is supreme.

And because its size is less unwieldy than that of the B.M. its staff is more fully acquainted with the details of its collection and has more time to be helpful. As at the B.M. the main catalogue is by authors and you can find things in it for yourself, but if you want early directories, old guide-books, parish registers or anything else that might be difficult to look up, you have only to explain your wants at the enquiry desk and the book you need, if they have it, is placed before you in a few minutes. If they don't have it they may suggest something else to serve the purpose. This is why the Guildhall Library can seem like balm to the exhausted searcher. No catalogue trouble, no waiting; no ticket required either, and no charge.

Of course you won't find your great-uncle's memoirs there or your great-aunt's little book of poems, but the more generally useful material for family history is readily available. If your forbears were Londoners this is the place to look for them, but its records are good for the whole country.

But there is yet another library in London that must be recommended as best of all for tracing ancestry, its only drawback being that you have to pay for it, the library of the **Society of Genealogists**. You need no recommendation, but may just walk in and use the library at once by paying for a day or half-day. (See page 122.) If you are going to be in or near London for some time you may decide that it is worth becoming a member, in which case your annual subscription will entitle you to other advantages besides the regular use of its splendid library.

This library consists only of books that might be useful for family history, and of these it has the largest collection in the country. There are of course some old books, long out of print, that can be found in the British Museum

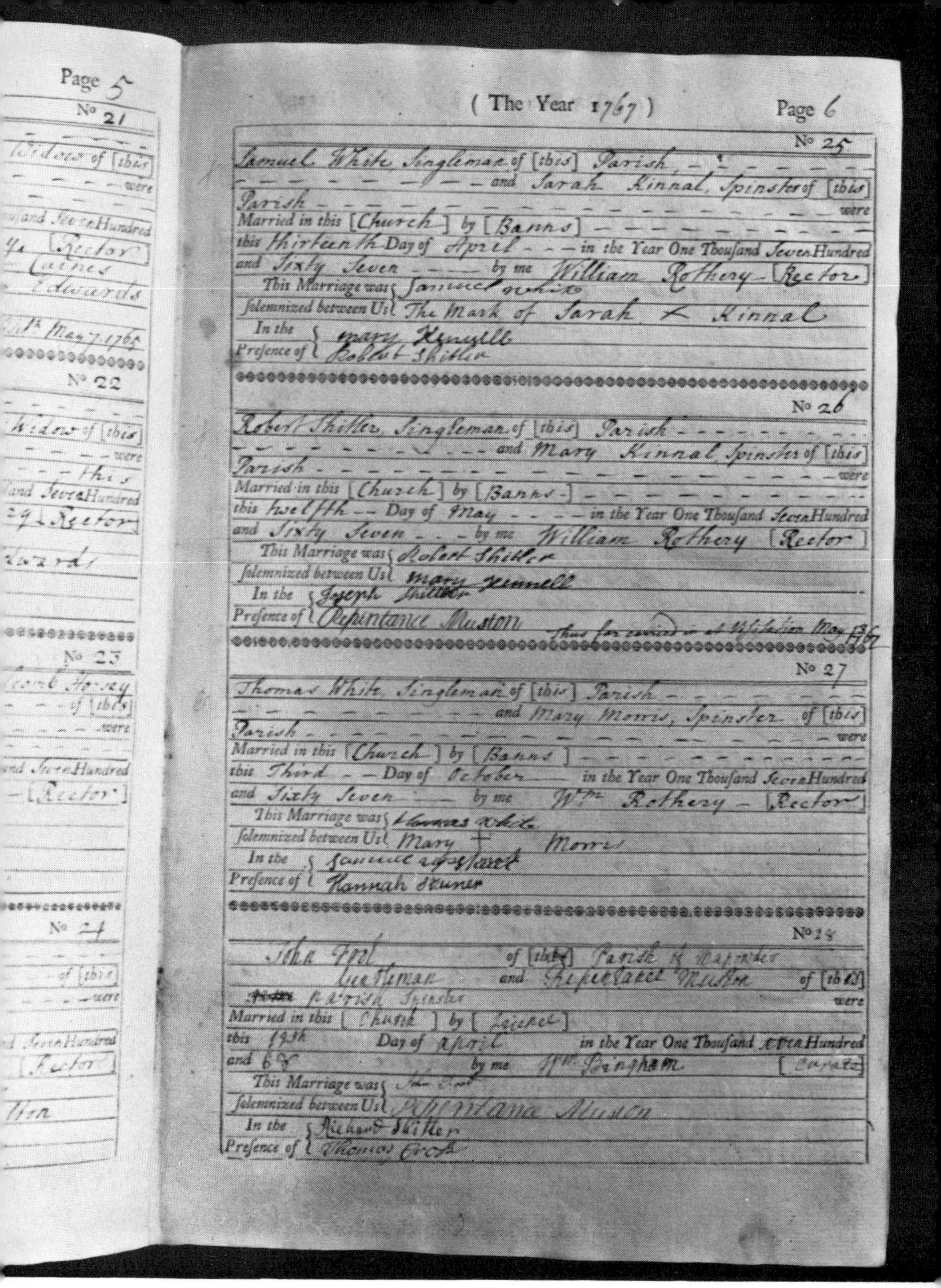

Plate 1 The marriage register of Hazelbury Bryan, 1767, showing the forms introduced in 1754

Note that Repentance Muston, who is a witness in the second entry and writes a good hand, marries Mr Foot, a gentleman, by licence in the bottom entry, whereas of the other three brides, all married by banns, two simply make their marks.

Marriages
1637.
Henry Lisse and Edith Numan married April 27.

Baptisms Anno Doi 1638
1638.
John the Sonne of John Baker Bapt. April 8th.
Johane Miller daughter of Thom: Miller Bapt. 4. June
Ralphe the Sonne of Stephan ffisher Bapt. 4th June
James the Sonne of Will: Shorte Bapt. 29th of Julie
Marie the daughter of Ralph Richman Bapt. 21 Aug
Jone the daughter of Roger ffifed Jun. Bapt. 23 octob
Margaret the daughter of John Woodman Bapt. 23 Decemb
Stephan the Sonne of Stephan Kelly Bapt. 2. ffebruary
Mathias the Sonne of Roger Jones Bapt. 13 of March.
Robert the Sonne of Edward Horner Bapt. 17 March.

1638 – Buriall.s
James Sonne of Stephan Kelly Buryed. 20th March
Willia the Sonne of Oliver Lilly Buried 18th of Aprill.
John Sonne of John Hust Buried the 19th of Aprill.
Edithe Newman vid. Buried the 22th of June.
Ralphe the Sonne of Ralph ffisher Buried 29 of June.
Mary the wife of Thomas Norris Buryed 26. July.
Giles Braffyld widdow Buried 12th of August.
Alice the wife of Richard marvile Buried 15 August.
Robert Lambert Buryed the 20th of August
Dorothy Cox was Buried the 23 day of August
Marie Durdale Buried the 30th day of August
Edithe the wife of John Masie Buryed 10th September
Agnes the wife of Edward Braffyld Buryed 16th Septemb
John the Sonne of John Baker Buried the same day 16 Sept
Emula Jones Soluta Sepult the 21th September
Edmund the Sonne of Luke King Buryed 29 September
John the wife of Charls Sorrell gent Buried 6. octob
Dorothy daughter of George ffisher Buryed 21. octob 1639

Plate 2 The parish register of Gussage All Saints, 1637–1638, with marriage, baptism and burial entries all on the same page

This vicar writes a nice italic hand, with occasional lapses into Secretary letters such as the capital C of Cox in the tenth burial entry. He is inconsistent, throwing in the odd word of Latin. as in the fifteenth entry with *soluta sepult* ('spinster, buried'), and gives even less information than usual in the baptism entries where he should give the names of both parents. Note that the New Year begins in March.

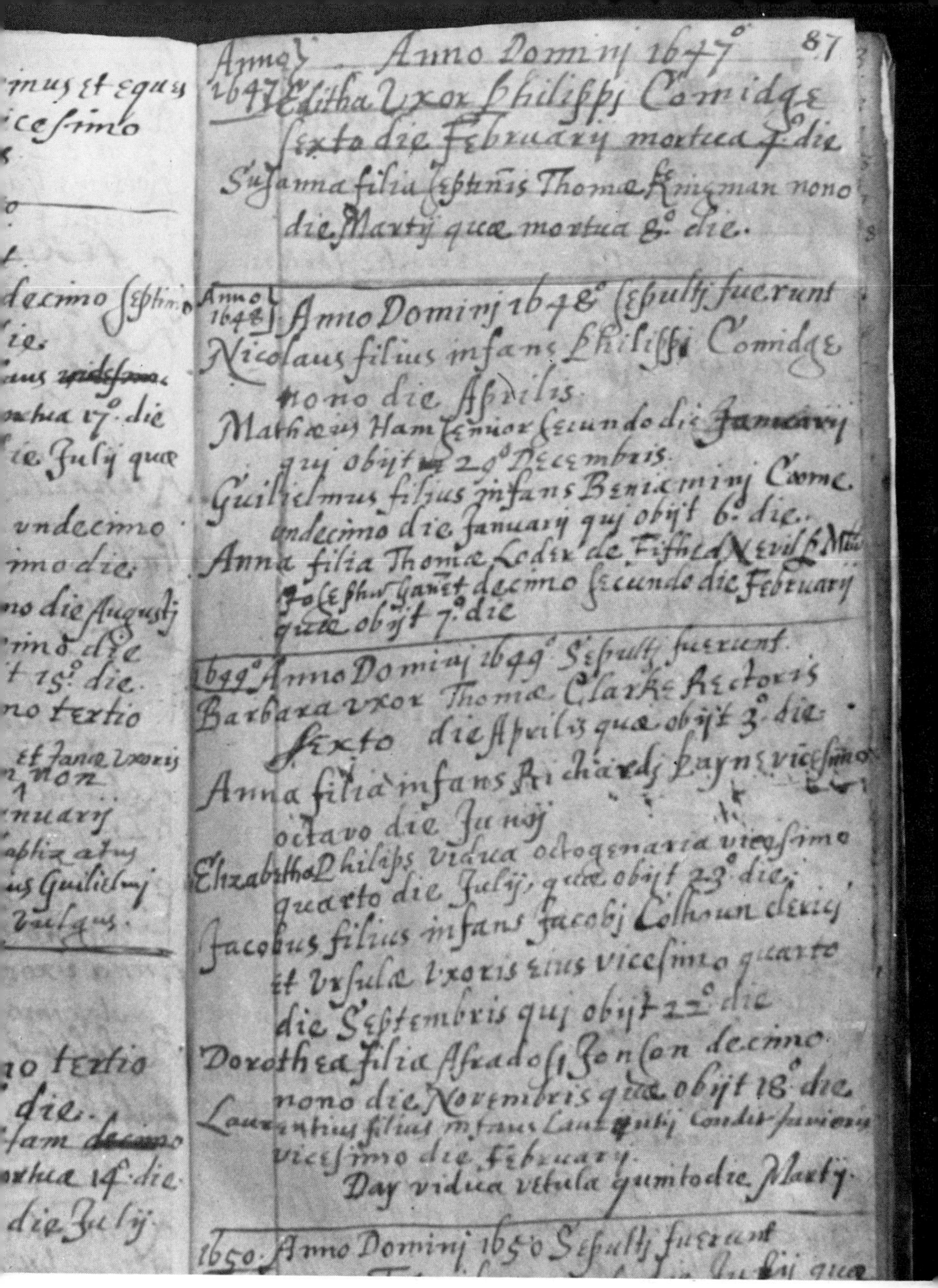

Anno 1647 Anno Domini 1647° 87

Editha Uxor Philipps Comidge sexto die February mortua 4° die

Susanna filia [illegible] Thomae Kingman nono die Martij quae mortua 8° die.

Anno 1648 Anno Domini 1648° sepulti fuerunt

Nicolaus filius infans Philippi Comidge nono die Aprilis

Mathaeus Ham senior secundo die Januarij qui obijt 29° Decembris.

Guilielmus filius infans Beniamini Crome undecimo die January qui obijt 6° die.

Anna filia Thomae Loder de Fifhead Nevill [illegible]

Josephus [illegible] decimo secundo die February quae obijt 7° die

1649° Anno Domini 1649° Sepulti fuerunt

Barbara uxor Thomae Clarke Rectoris sexto die Aprilis quae obijt 3° die

Anna filia infans Richardi Payne vicesimo octavo die Junij

Elizabetha Philipps vidua octogenaria vicesimo quarto die Julij, quae obijt 23° die

Jacobus filius infans Jacobi Colhoun clerici et Ursulae Uxoris eius vicesimo quarto die Septembris qui obijt 22° die

Dorothea filia [illegible] Jonson decimo nono die Novembris quae obijt 18° die

Laurentius filius infans [illegible] junioris vicesimo die February.

Day vidua vetula quinto die Martij

1650 Anno Domini 1650 Sepulti fuerunt

Plate 3 The burials register of Hazelbury Bryan, 1647–1650

This vicar, writing in Latin, would appear to be more scholarly and careful than the last. He is certainly more informative, saying, for example, in the third entry 'Nicholas, infant son of Philip Comidge' and in the ninth 'Elizabeth Philips, octogenarian widow', and frequently giving the date of death as well as the date of burial. Note that in the last entry for 1649 he has left a space, evidently hoping to fill in the Christian name of the Widow Day who was buried on the fifth of March.

Plate 4   The Poor Book of Melbury Osmond with the accounts for April, 1732

On the right-hand side is a list of the village inhabitants, headed by 'The Honble Thos Strang-ways Horner Esq.' who has a whole string of properties, stating the amount each household is to pay for the relief of the poor, 'to be collected monthly or as often as Need Shall Require'. Most of the sums are very small. On the left-hand side is the record of disbursements, with Samuel Wheatam 'in his Lameness' and Hezekiah Chiles 'in his need' receiving various small sums, while 'ye Soldiers Boy and Andrews Boy' are equipped with breeches, stockings and mended 'Cloaths'.

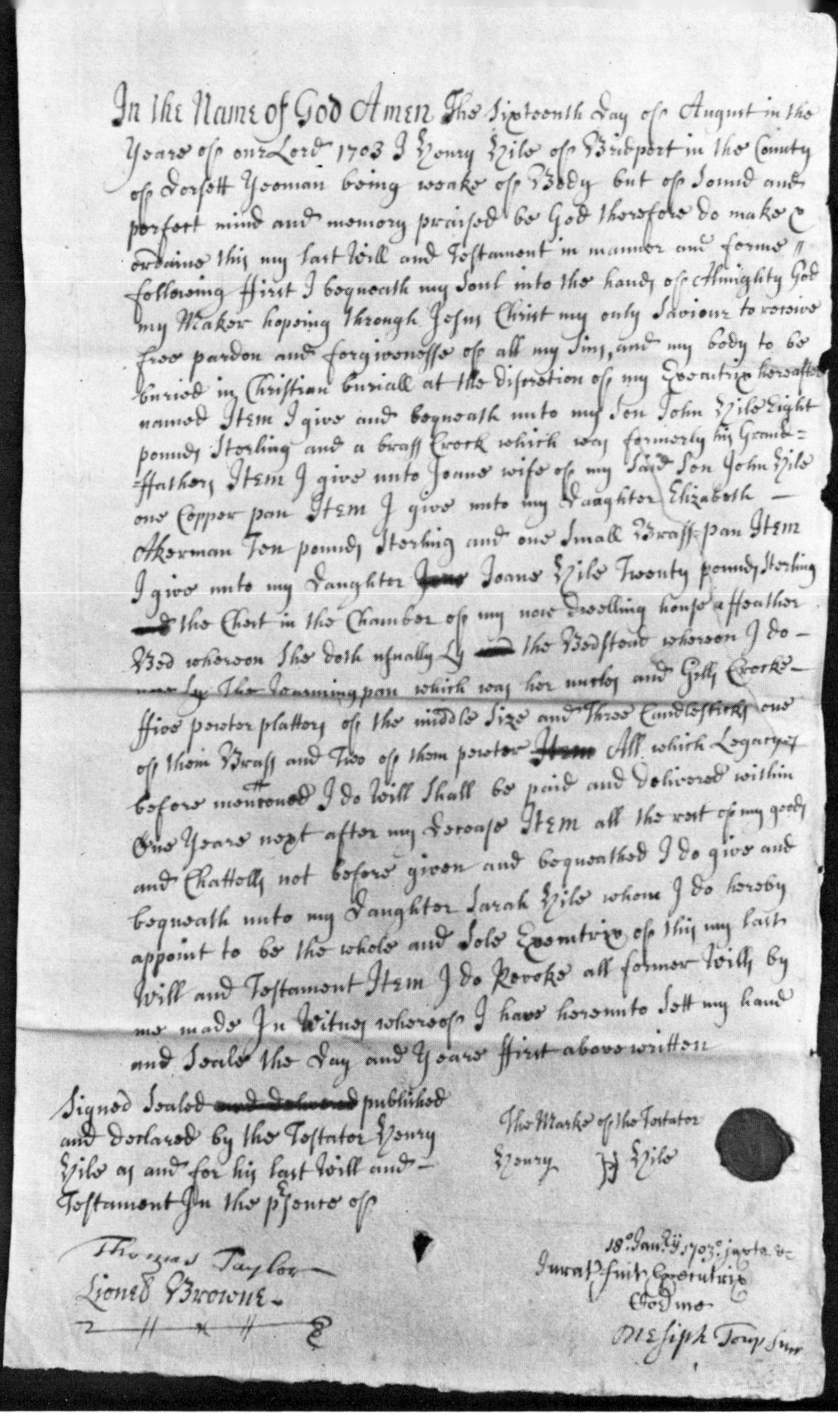

Plate 5 The Will of Henry Hile, yeoman, of Bridport, 1703 (now in the Dorset County Record Office)

The opening lines of this Will are standard. The bequests begin on line 10 with 'Item I give and bequeath unto my Son John Hile Eight pounds Sterling and a brass Crock which was formerly his Grandfathers'. Note the Secretary 'r' and 'c' in 'Crock', looking like a modern 'w' and 'r' respectively. A transcription of this Will appears in Appendix C on page 121. The testator's mark is more elaborate and individual than the usual X. A typical yeoman's Will.

At the Court Leet and View of ffrank pledge with the Court Baron of the Right Honourable Stephen [ ] Earl of Ilchester Lord Ilchester and Staverdale Baron Strangways of Woodsford Strangways in the County of Dorset and Baron of Redlynch in the County of Somerset Lord of the said Liberty and Manor there held on ffriday the 2d day of October in the Seventh Year of the Reign of our Sovereign Lord George the Third now King of Great Britain and so forth and in the Year of our Lord 1767

Constable there	William Ansty
Dewlish Tythingman	William ffoot
Milborn Church Town Tythingman	James Harding } appear
Hayward	William ffoot

The Names of the Jury and Homage

William Alner		John Roberts	
Richard Draper	sworn	William Oxford	
John Vincent Son?		Edward Vincent	
John Ansty		Thomas Williams	sworn found and present
David Drake	sworn	Robert ffoot	as follows to wit
William Alner Sen.		and	
William Dall		Arthur Anthony	

First We present that the Heirs of Sr John Moreton Barronett the Heirs of Sr James Long Barronett the Representative of the late Thomas Skinner Esqr and Thomas Gundrey Esqr are ffreeholders within this Manor and owe Suite and Service to this Court but have made default of their appearance here this day for which we amerce each and every of them 2s 0

Also We present that the Copyhold Tenants can by the custom of this Manor lop or Top such Trees as have been formerly lopped or topped for ffirewood and can also have the Wood trees and hollow Trees and decayed Windfalls for ffirewood without leave of the Lord on our own Tenements without making wast or sale thereof

Also We present upon notice given to the Lord of this Manor or His Steward or Bailiff of the occasion for cutting of Timber for repairing Houses or Tenements the same to be allowed and assigned or in default thereof after such notice given then the Tenants may take the same provided he doth not sell the same nor make any wast or destruction thereof

Also We present that by our Custome We can let our Copyhold Tenements for one Year and a day and no longer

Also We present that on the death or surrender or forfeiture of every Copyhold Tenant being possessed of a Copyhold Tenement there is an Heriot due to the Lord of the said Manor which is the best Beast or Goods of such Tenant dying

Plate 6 The Manorial Court Book of Dewlish, 1767 (see pages 85–7)

In this court book, the Homage precedes the Default of Tenants, which begins 'First We present that the Heirs of Sr John Moreton Barronett –'. This is followed by statements of the customs of the manor: the first declares 'We present that the Copyhold Tenants can by the custom of this Manor lop or Top such Trees as have been formerly lopped or topped for Firewood and can also have the Wood trees and hollow Trees and decayed Windfalls for Firewood without leave of the Lord on our own Tenements without making wast or sale thereof.'

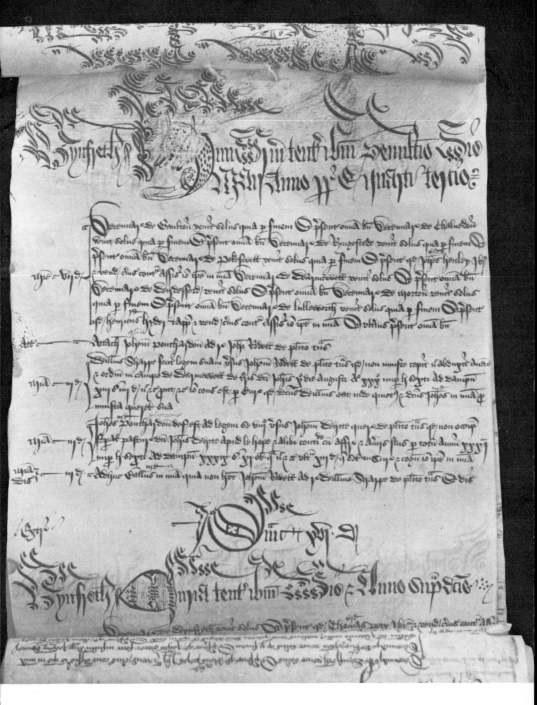

Plate 7 A Court Roll of Wynfrith Hundred, 1463

An extreme example of exuberant capitals and abbreviated Latin, written by a legal scribe who evidently took pride in his work. The heading reads *'Wynfreth Hundr̄m tent' ib̄m penultimo Die Maii anno rr E quarti tertio'* [if the abbreviated words were spelt out, this would read: *Wynfreth Hundredum tentum ibidem penultimo Die Maii anno regni regis Edwardi quarti tertio*] which may be translated 'Wynfrith Hundred Court held here on the penultimate day of May in the third year of the reign of King Edward IV'.

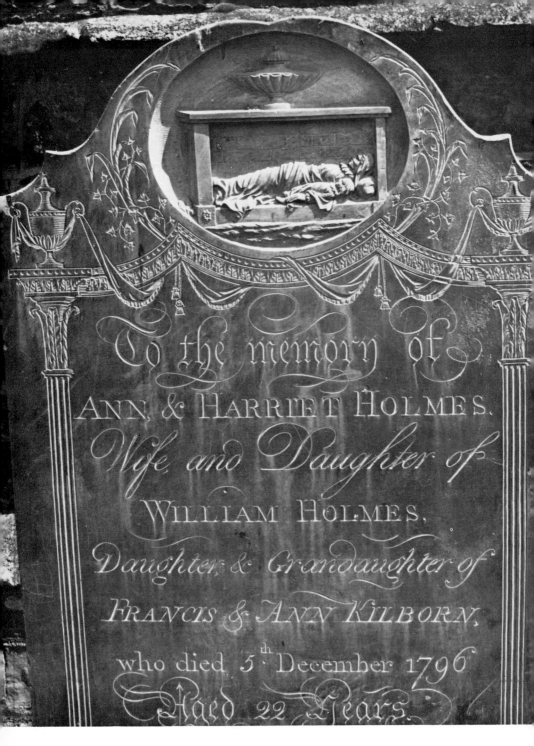

Plate 8 The gravestone of Ann Holmes and her daughter Harriet, 1796, at Desborough

This is an example of a memorial inscription which tells us more than the parish register would do, for the names of Ann Holmes's parents, who very likely erected the stone, are given as prominently as that of her husband.

or Guildhall libraries but not here, but to set against that the Genealogists have a great collection of records in typescript that have never been published and can be found here only. There are, for instance, not only copies of all the parish registers that have ever been printed but many more as well that have been industriously copied by members of the Society. They are arranged by counties and readily available.

An outstanding example of the kind of work of which a visitor to this library can take full advantage is the *Boyd Marriage Index* which consists of entries from marriage registers from all parts of the country from the Tudor period to 1837. They are mostly arranged by counties in chronological order, and each volume (covering twenty-five years) is indexed, so that sitting comfortably at a table near the shelves, you can rapidly cover a wide area of time and space. This is invaluable if you are trying to locate an elusive family. This great work is unfortunately incomplete; it does not include all counties or every parish in any county, but there is enough of it to increase considerably your chances of finding the whereabouts of a missing family. It has been calculated that about seven million people are indexed.

A much larger, and even more valuable, index is the *C.F.I.*, which has already been described (page 44). As mentioned there, it already contains over 32,000,000 entries, and work on it is going on all the time.

Another typescript collection of great value is an *Index of Apprentices Indentures* for the whole of England and Wales from 1710 to 1774. This gives a useful cross-section of ordinary people, for the names both of apprentices and masters are indexed with their home town and occupation. It is this sort of thing that puts the Genealogists' Library in a class by itself.

But perhaps its chief merit is the freedom one enjoys to find everything for oneself. All the books and all the typed collections are available on the shelves for the visitor to help himself to. There is no waiting; you may consult volume after volume at your fancy, finding useful books that you didn't know existed. And the range is extremely wide. There are sections not only for each county, but also for Welsh, Scottish and Irish records, and for those of America and many parts of the Commonwealth.

In my opinion it is worth the money.

9

Occupations and Professions

Among the bits of tradition that are passed down in families there is often something about a profession. 'My grandfather's people were all in the church', or 'I believe his grandfather made boots in Nottingham.' Such remarks are often inaccurate. Ancestors may be promoted to higher ranks than any they really held or conversely disparaged in a determination not to be snobbish. Likewise a man's occupation may be found in a will or other legal document, in which case it will be more reliable; but however it comes such information is always a useful pointer.

As regards a **trade** or **craft**—like the bootmaking—much depends on being able to locate it. Then you can try the borough or city library of that district and see what they have on local trades. As libraries vary so much in what they have of this sort and the possible occupations are innumerable, little more can be said except a word of encouragement, for you may be surprised at the records that do exist. If you don't know the locality it may be worth trying the Index of Apprentices in the Genealogists' Library (page 65) for that covers the whole country.

If one of your ancestors is described in some document as 'Citizen of London', generally with a trade specified as for instance 'Citizen and Fishmonger', it means that he was a member of one of the city livery companies, and these all have a wealth of old records—unless they were destroyed in the last war. You can best find out about them at the Guildhall Library (page 64). But don't picture the ancestor selling fish in person; the words imply that he was a rich merchant, probably living in grander style than many a poor 'gentleman' in the country.

Turning to the professions—we think first of **the church**. The standard reference book on the clergy, Crockford's Directory, was first published in 1858. Before that there is no comprehensive list but many different sources. Joseph Foster's *Index Ecclesiasticus* gives details of parsons between 1800 and 1840 but it is a rare book and not to be seen in many libraries. However as almost all the clergy had university degrees, one can get at them through the university registers which are also invaluable source books for thousands of young men of good family. The same Joseph Foster, a great genealogist who made many collections, edited *Alumni Oxoniensis* giving particulars of all those who entered Oxford from 1500 to 1886. The corresponding compilation for Cambridge, *Alumni Cantabridgiensis*, which runs from the start of the university to 1900, was made by John Venn and J. A. Venn. Both these important works give dates of matriculation—when the young man was about 16 so one can calculate the date of birth approximately—and other useful biographical details.

Until Durham was founded in 1832 (and London in 1836) Oxford and Cambridge were the only English universities, but Scotland had four old ones, St Andrews (1411), Glasgow (1451), Aberdeen (1494) and Edinburgh (1483). So if you fail to find your parson or scholar at Oxford or Cambridge it is worth looking for him there, especially if he lived in the north of England. Their lists of matriculations and graduates are not so full or so easily come by as the English ones but they all have some which you can find with a little persistence.

Another possibility for locating a university man is Trinity College, Dublin, founded in 1591. You may think your family would not send a son there unless they had an Irish connection, but for people living in the west, especially if near a port, it was nearer than Oxford. From Liverpool, for instance, the short sea crossing was both easier and cheaper than the long coach journey.

Records of ordinations and appointments to benefices are contained in the Bishops Registers which are kept in Diocesan Libraries. A few of these are still separate repositaries of church records in cathedral cities, but most of them have been amalgamated with their local city or county record office.

Once you have located your parson as a parish priest you will find him in its register recording events of his own family as well as those of others, and you can often form a strong personal impression from the way he kept his register; whether he was scholarly (using Latin), artistic (writing beautifully), untidy (blots and smudges), sympathetic ('buried Thomas the sonne of Mr Walker a pritty ingenius and hopeful yonge child'), or lazy (leaving it all to an ignorant clerk). Even in the last case you will see his signature at intervals, and the recording of his death or departure which may draw a comment from his successor. Thomas Hassall, who became vicar of Great Amwell (Herts) in 1590 noted that his predecessor was 'a man very unworthy simple and negligent'. On his own death someone wrote *Non erat ante nec erit postea te similis* ('There never was or will be again anyone like you').

We come next to **the law**. From the Middle Ages onward it was customary for young men of good family to be enrolled—as an alternative to the university—at one of the four Inns of Court in London, and it was only through them that one could qualify as a barrister or for any of the higher legal appointments. So here again the best way to find a lawyer before the nineteenth century is through their registers of admissions. Those of Grays Inn are edited by the same John Foster who published the Oxford records; the registers of the Middle Temple will be found in library catalogues under the name of H. A. C. Sturgess, while those of Lincoln's Inn are listed under its name. For the Inner Temple you must write to its librarian.

The lower ranks of the legal profession, solicitors and attorneys, are more elusive. Such men generally had their training as clerks, working for those already qualified, and the best hope of finding them in the eighteenth century is in the Apprenticeship Index which runs from 1710 to 1774. Soon after that *Browne's Law Lists* began publication. The B.M. has them (indexed under *Directories*) from 1777 and the Guildhall Library from slightly later. But they give little except names and addresses.

The medical profession is less well documented than you might expect or hope. Its history is complicated by the fact that before the nineteenth century it was not one profession but three. In the highest categories were the physicians who, according to a law of 1522, must have university degrees. So they may be looked for like the clergy in the Oxford and Cambridge registers. But in this field the Scottish universities led the way, and by the mid-eighteenth century Glasgow, Edinburgh and Aberdeen had medical schools that many Englishmen attended. Others took degrees in Dublin or abroad.

Surgeons were considered socially inferior to physicians. In 1640 they were united in a City Company with the Barbers but about a century later broke away and gradually obtained more recognition. It was in the many wars of the eighteenth century that their services came to be better valued and those who served with the Army, Navy or East India Company are much easier to trace than those who stayed at home. We will come to these service records presently. At home they learned their trade chiefly from someone already in practice, and so again the Apprenticeship Index is a place in which to look for them. But the urge towards healing is often hereditary, and if a boy learned from his father or through a private arrangement with a relation there is no way of tracing it.

The men to whom most people turned for help in their ailments were the apothecaries, who also rose in general esteem during the eighteenth century. They too may be found as apprentices but they had their own guild, which issued licences to practise and these—from about 1780—may be seen at the Guildhall Library.

By the early nineteenth century these three bodies of men were beginning to converge together. Both physicians and surgeons often qualified also as apothecaries (so they may be found in those licences just mentioned) and the general practitioner was at last emerging. If you are looking for a doctor in a particular district an early directory of that locality may help you. In 1845 the *Medical Directory of Great Britain and Ireland* began to appear but it is not as comprehensive as its title suggests. The official *Medical Register* (like Crockford's *Directory of the Clergy*) began in 1858.

When we turn to **the armed services** the picture is much brighter for the researcher. Indeed the mass of material available is so great that the difficulty lies more in finding one's way about it than in any lack of information.

Some of the more recent army records are kept at the General Register Office, but the bulk of them are at the P.R.O. at Kew, classed as War Office (WO). Naval Records (Admiralty, ADM) are there too. If your ancestors were officers, you should with any luck be able to reconstruct their full careers from the printed Army and Navy lists (which begin in the mid-18th century) and the standard works in the P.R.O. reference room (see Book List, page 118, Fortescue, and 119, O'Byrne). But it is never hard to trace distinguished men. The great strength of the P.R.O. is that it records the undistinguished too. In its vast mass of unpublished material are the names of even the lowest ranks of soldiers and sailors, if only you can find them, men who in their own day were often classed as the scum of society.

The records are so voluminous that it is wise to go prepared. Ask in advance if there is a P.R.O. leaflet on the subject you want, or try the book *Tracing Your Ancestors in the P.R.O.* (see page 118, Cox). A specialist genealogical work, such as *In Search of Army Ancestry*, by Gerald Hamilton-Edwards is invaluable.

At Kew there are two modern reading rooms, Langdale and Romilly, with a reference room between them. All seats are numbered. Reserve one at the Langdale distribution counter, collect the bleeper for that seat number, and move on to the Reference Room. The staff at the enquiry desk will help you to find the reference numbers for the records you want. Put in your order, either by computer (very quick) or by filling in a slip; then you are free to browse until your bleeper summons you to Langdale to collect your records and take them to your seat.

As always in research you must know some key fact before you can learn more. For the army you need to know the regiment; for the navy you want the name of the ship. This may seem an impossible hurdle to overcome, but if you have heard that your ancestor fought in some battle (and this is just the sort of thing that is remembered) you can find out from military and naval histories which regiments or which ships took part in the engagement, and work your way through the muster rolls at Kew. It is a long job, but it can be done.

Some of my own family research will serve as an example of the kind of obscure details that can be unearthed with a little persistence. My great-grandfather, Nicholas Carrington, gained some passing fame in his own day as a minor poet and wrote a short memoir in which he said that his father had been employed at Plymouth Dock, where he too was apprenticed as a boy. We used fondly to imagine the father, Henry, in a rather good position, probably clerical, and when we found his marriage certificate in the Dockyard parish church (1775) it was a surprise to see him described as a sawyer. After that it hardly seemed worth looking for Dockyard records. They could hardly mention a manual worker of two hundred years ago.

But the Naval Dockyards are part of the Establishment and eventually I did look for their archives among the Admiralty records and found Henry Carrington. There he was in a Description Book of 1779, complete with his age and years of service, married with one child, character good, height 5 ft 6 ins, complexion fresh, but somewhat pockmarked. In the case of an aristocratic ancestor one might hope to see a portrait, but to have this working man to whom I partly owe my own life set before me so plainly gave me quite a turn. What if he had not survived the smallpox?

I am glad to say that he didn't spend all his life sawing hearts of oak for our ships. It must have been very hard work. He contracted out and built up a business of his own, supplying timber and other goods to the Dockyard. But he qualified for a pension of which the records are there, with his signature every quarter, and this gave me the date of his death which I had failed to find elsewhere.

He apprenticed his son, Nicholas, to a 'measurer' in the Dockyard, presumably to measure the timber for ship-building which was one stage better than sawing it. But the boy, whose mind was steeped in books and poetry (surely this throws some light on the sawyer's home life) hated the Dockyard and his 'ruffianly companions' and ran away to sea, enlisting on a naval ship, where he could hardly have found the company below decks much more refined. He took part in the battle of Cape St Vincent, about which he wrote a poem, and this fact gave us the clue to look through the Muster Rolls of all the English ships in the battle. We found him as a carpenter's mate (very suitable) and later in a collection of Seamen's Wills (in the same department) I found the one he had made when he went on board, leaving all his possessions—which must have been about nil—'to my beloved father, Henry Carrington' from whom he had run away.

After that adventure Nicholas soon came out of the navy, was reunited with his family and gained enough success as a writer to win himself a place in the *Dictionary of National Biography*. But (strangely) they got his name wrong, calling him Noel instead of Nicholas, which goes to show that you can't believe everything you see in printed books—even the most impressive of them. Original records written by hand in the presence of the man concerned are the real thing.

The P.R.O. also holds detailed collections of records of **the Marines**, and of **the Merchant Navy**, including Ships Logs, Masters' Certificates and so on. To describe these there is a free leaflet available called *The Mercantile Marine*. Again there is a mass of material.

And while we are thinking of soldiers and sailors we should bear in mind that before 1858 the rich and powerful **East India Company** had its own army and navy and body of administrators entirely separate from the national services. Their officers both on sea and land used the same system of ranks and titles as those of the royal forces but they will not be found in the records of the War Office or Admiralty. However, everything undertaken by the East India Company was well organized and their archives are no exception. Among the many printed registers of officers and civilians several of the most useful are compiled by Dodwell and Miles and you can find these under their names in the larger libraries. There is also D. J. Crawford's *Roll of the Indian Medical Service 1615–1930* of which there is no counterpart for doctors at home. Charles Hardy's *Register of Ships of the E.I.C.* is also useful and the *East India Register and Directory* which was published annually from 1803 to 1895. For more information write to the India Office Records (page 134).

I was once engaged on the history of a house in the country which changed hands in 1787. The name of the new owner, 'Stephen Williams Esq', was on the deed of sale but I had no notion as to the sort of man he was or where he had come from. Then in one of the Vestry books of the parish I saw a reference to 'Captain Williams' and that was the clue I needed. My first idea was to go through Army Lists and Navy Lists, but though there were plenty of officers of appropriate dates called Williams not one of them in either service was a Stephen (a name that was not much used at that time). Next I bethought me of the East India Service and there he was, a captain in their fleet, just retired. Having pinned him down I was soon able to unearth his whole career and background—for his father had been in the same service—and came to feel that I knew him intimately; and all because of the word 'Captain'.

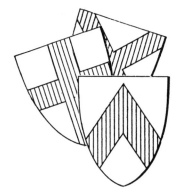

IO

Rank and Heraldry

In old documents you often see a man described as 'gentleman' or 'esquire' and these terms, though never very exactly defined, were clearly understood by everybody.

On the whole, 'gentlemen' belonged to the land-owning and official classes. The word 'esquire' implied a greater distinction—the eldest son of a knight or manorial lord, or an officer above a certain rank. Most of them, though not all, were entitled by their birth to bear heraldic arms.

Everyone knows these attractive-looking shields each bearing a heraldic device associated with a particular family but there is also a good deal of confusion and misunderstanding on the subject.

The system arose in the twelfth and thirteenth centuries when every man of the upper classes expected some fighting in his life and a shield was a practical part of his personal equipment. He won the rank of knighthood in actual battle, fighting on horseback fully armed, and as his face was then concealed by his helmet he had a bold design painted on his shield so that his friends and followers could recognize him. The same design was embroidered by his womenfolk on the *cotte* or loose tunic that he wore over his armour, hence the term **coat of arms**.

Knighthood meant much more than courage and skill in battle. It was linked with a code of conduct expressed in the word 'chivalry' in which military prowess must be matched by courtesy and gentleness. Chaucer's knight 'loved truth and honour' and was 'a very perfect gentle knight'; and it was this word 'gentle' that was most often applied to knightly behaviour at its best.

The title of knight was never hereditary; it was something each man must win for himself; but the rank of gentility (a word that has been ruined in modern times) did pass on to all his descendants, and with it the right to use his coat of arms as an outward sign of their knightly origin. At home these 'gentlemen' or 'gentry' were mostly landowners, some in a small way, but all sharing with the nobility and royalty above them the right to heraldic arms.

Times grew more peaceful but pride in these inherited honours in no way decreased. They were carved in stone, engraved on silver, woven in tapestry, set up in stained glass, and used as the chief ornament of funeral monuments. And all the time they kept on growing more elaborate. When a man married an heiress of gentle blood he could, if he chose, combine his arms with hers by *impaling* them, that is placing them side by side. Their children would then use a *quartered* shield with their father's arms in two diagonally placed quarters and their mother's in the other two. Some families that made many important marriages showed them in extremely complicated quartering, but when a shield becomes too elaborate it ceases to be effective and some distinguished families have preferred the simpler arms of earlier times.

Another complication was that, strictly speaking, the inherited arms belonged to the head of the family only, all sons and daughters being supposed to place some small *difference* upon them to denote the relationship; but when the heir succeeded the difference was removed. This accounts for the way in which different branches of the same family bear arms that are basically the same but with some variation. However this system has not been carried out consistently.

Impalement (above) Quartering (below)

Set out in its full glory each whole arrangement of arms or *achievement* as it is called, consists of the shield (or *escutcheon*) flanked by two fanciful figures, often of birds or animals (the *supporters*) and surmounted by another emblem, known as the *crest*. This was supposed to represent the object worn on the helmet in battle as another point of recognition. It might take the form of a beast or bird or part of one, but could in fact be anything. Because the crest was generally a simpler affair than the shield it was often used in later times as an alternative family emblem. In the nineteenth century it was fashionable to have one's crest embossed on one's note paper and the common error arose of using the

word 'crest' when what was meant was the shield
or coat of arms.

Below the shield the family *motto* is shown on a
gracefully curving scroll. These may be in Norman
French, Latin or English and are often very old.
The best known achievement of arms is that of the
Queen, in which the supporters are a lion and
unicorn, the crest a crowned lion (often simplified
to a crown only), and the motto *Dieu et mon droit*.

**Lions from the royal
arms, passant guard-
ant (above), rampant
(below)**

Every art and craft has its own technical terms,
its special jargon which the newcomer must master
to avoid appearing grossly ignorant, but none has
a more particular language of its own than heraldry.
Because it first developed at a time when the court
and nobility spoke Norman French it is based
chiefly on that language but mixed with English
so that the result is a curious hotch-potch.

For those who are deeply interested there are
several standard works available (see page 117),
but if you want only a simple introduction to the
rudiments of **heraldic language** here is a short
basic vocabulary.

The main surface of the shield is called the *field*.
Its upper part is the *chief*. The right-hand side—
from the point of view of the bearer—is the
dexter; the left side being the *sinister*.

The arms are depicted in strong, clear colours:
gules (red), *azure* (blue), *sable* (black), *vert* (green)
and *purpure* (purple).

There are also two metals: *or* (gold) and *argent*
(silver). In painted arms they are represented by
yellow and white, but you mustn't call them that.
And there are two furs, *ermine* and *vair*, which are
shown as stylized patterns.

Anything that is depicted on the shield is called
a *charge*. The oldest and most basic of these are
simple geometrical patterns known as *ordinaries*.
They consist of:

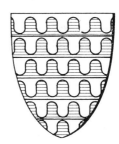

**Vair (above)
Ermine (below)**

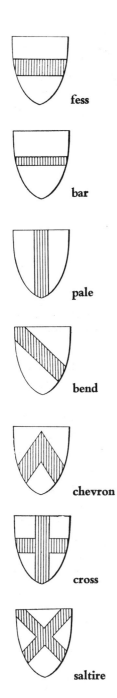

fess

bar

pale

bend

chevron

cross

saltire

a *fess*	a broad horizontal band
a *bar*	a similar one but narrower
a *pale*	a vertical band
a *bend*	a diagonal band from dexter chief to sinister base; *bend sinister* went the other way and implied illegitimacy
a *chevron*	two bands slanting upwards and meeting in a point
a *cross*	the plainest kind; those of other styles have special names
a *saltire*	a diagonal cross

From the first beginnings of heraldry some stylized pictures of fierce animals appeared among these simple shapes, and as time passed shields were charged with more and more symbolical objects and creatures of every sort. Some are described in plain words, but many by special heraldic terms. For instance, a five-pointed star is a *mullet* and a small circle or roundel is a *torteaux*. There are special words for the attitudes of heraldic beasts. The lions on the royal arms of England are *passant guardant* which means that they are walking with their heads turned towards us. But the lion of Scotland is *rampant*, that is, on its hind legs.

When a shield is described it is said to be *blazoned*, and the correct way to do it is exact and economical of words. You must begin with the field and one word is generally enough unless it is patterned all over. For instance *checky, argent and gules* means that the whole shield is checked in white and red. *Bendy, or and azure* means that it is covered with alternate gold and blue diagonal stripes.

After stating the nature of the field, you proceed to give the charges, the adjective always following the noun. To take a simple but effective shield showing a white chevron on a blue ground, the correct blazon would be *azure, a chevron argent.* The arms of the Washington family from whom George Washington was descended might be described by the uninitiated as a white shield with two red stripes across the middle and three red stars above them. The correct blazon is *argent, two bars and in chief three mullets gules.* Heralds do not use more words than the minimum, and the adjective *gules* applies to *bars* as well as *mullets.*

The Washington Arms

Although in theory all armorial families were descended from knights, this class distinction was not rigidly maintained in England. Merchants, craftsmen and yeomen who had grown rich and built themselves fine houses could apply to the **College of Heralds** for grants of arms and if successful be accepted as gentlemen. Eyebrows might be raised by those who prided themselves on their own knightly blood and held that true gentility could not be bought, but if the newcomers lived like gentlemen they were soon accepted as such.

This brings us to the heralds who decided upon such matters. Many people are not clear about who they were—or are—for there are still heralds today, the ultimate arbiters on matters of genealogy. To begin with they were officials employed by the king or great nobles to make formal announcements and sometimes to act on their lord's behalf. They wore their masters' arms on their clothing to show their special relationship to them, and at tournaments and other public events they took charge of the ceremonies, proclaiming the styles and titles of the contestants, and upholding all the traditional pomp. We still see them doing it at modern royal functions.

The whole business of coats of arms with all their trappings which had grown up spontaneously in the middle ages had become so complicated by the fifteenth century that an official body was needed to regulate it; and since the chief experts in this field were the heralds, the task of supervision was given to them. Thus the College of Heralds, founded in 1484, became the chief authority on family history and still is. And if you have reason to believe that some of your forbears used a crest or coat of arms and want to establish from that exactly who they were and where they came from you can write to the College of Arms who will investigate the matter for you with professional skill, and the use of old records not available to the public—for a fee. Or you can try to do it for yourself.

There are several standard works of reference that will help you to identify armorial families with which you might be connected. The most important are the works of Burke and of Fox-Davies as listed on page 118. Burke's *General Armoury*, for instance, includes past as well as present coats of arms. Here you can look up the surnames that concern you and see if a family of that name ever bore arms. There may be more than one and you should not assume you are descended from any of them without some good evidence. If your grandfather had a signet ring with the arms of one of them on it then at least you have a significant clue. But it must be admitted that more than one ambitious Victorian who aspired to be accepted among the 'county' families took just that easy course of finding out an old armorial family with the same name as his own and adopting its arms without more enquiry. If you are conscientious about your researches you will want to be satisfied that his action was justified.

When you consult reference books on the nobility and gentry there is no need to be discouraged because the main line of a family is said to be extinct. Every family had its less distinguished branches which the genealogists knew nothing of or preferred to ignore. Prodigal sons were no rarity and many never returned. Young men left home and failed to keep in touch, and often never bothered to use coats of arms or other traditional marks of gentility to which they might have been entitled. Many very ordinary people today are descended from armorial families and know nothing of it.

Most people's ancestry, if only they knew it, is very mixed. Printed pedigrees tend to be highly selective following the lines that lead to the most noble ancestors and ignoring the others. This may be condemned as snobbish but it is very understandable, for noble ancestors are much easier to trace than lesser folk. Once you can truly and honestly attach yourself to an armorial family you can probably find printed pedigrees that will take you back several generations—along the more creditable lines—without further trouble to yourself.

It was early in the nineteenth century that the great works on genealogy such as Burke's *Peerage* began to appear, but the study and glorification of ancestry was an established practice long before that. In the reign of Henry VIII a process was started, with a view to sorting out true claims from false, in which officials from the College of Heralds visited the different parts of the land, county by county, to investigate all claims to hereditary arms and this continued sporadically for more than a century. The results of these **Heralds' Visitations**, as they are called, have been published in many volumes by the Harleian Society and may be seen in the larger libraries. The hundreds of old pedigrees they contain form one of the main sources from which Burke and others obtained their material. They were also used by the antiquarians who began to produce county histories from the eighteenth century onwards in large and handsome volumes, designed to grace the libraries of country gentlemen.

In the interests of truth it must be said that modern genealogists tend to be sceptical about many of those old pedigrees that were supplied to rich patrons in the days when standards of scholarship were not as high as they are now and the wish to please was strong. 'The making of false pedigrees,' says Sir Anthony Wagner in his classic book *English Genealogy*, 'is an immemorial vice —— and the age of Elizabeth I has a specially bad name for such activities.' However, descents supplied by the heralds of that period are usually reliable for several generations back from the time they were written, for they had to satisfy the knowledge of old people still living. It is their earlier stages going back to romantic-sounding barons of the time of the Conquest that are suspect. *Domesday Book*, compiled in 1086, is a factual work which names the landowners of that date in a way that can be completely relied on; but from the following century few detailed records have survived, and few indeed of the old noble families can bridge the gap. It used to be fashionable for people to say that their ancestors 'came over with the Conqueror', but only the merest handful—three or four families—can prove such a thing. Personally I would rather be descended from the Saxons, and in fact all of us with English blood must be descended from one side or other and almost certainly from both.

Sometimes these heraldic pedigrees show descents from royalty and these are more generally trustworthy than those from early Norman barons. The one family in England that has an unbroken and unassailable descent from long before the Conquest is the royal family. At many points in its long history the daughters or younger sons of kings have married into the nobility and their children spread the net wider. Those of the aristocracy who boasted royal blood tended to marry each other but when families were large there were always some who married beneath them in rank and their descendants multiplied. Edward III had a particularly large and prolific family and it was calculated early in this century that his descendants must then be approaching 100,000. So if you find a pedigree linking your family with royalty there is no need to distrust it on that account. The compilers of family histories could and did make up fictitious barons, but they couldn't invent sons and daughters for English kings since the Conquest and hope to get away with it. The enjoyable thing about establishing a link of this sort

is that you have your share in the royal ancestry from that time back including many famous figures, good and bad. But keep your sense of proportion.
Remember the vast number of ancestors we each have—and share—in
distant times. It is nice to know that Alfred the Great was one of them, but
don't forget all the nameless peasants ploughing the soil, for we all have
plenty of those in our ancestry too.

The pedigree on the opposite page is an example of a royal descent to an
ordinary middle-class family. Margaret Warner (at the bottom) was my
mother's grandmother, a formidable old lady—as my mother remembered
her—and greatly conscious of her dignity. In modest circumstances, she was
buoyed up by the knowledge of her ancestry, not so much the link with
royalty illustrated here as the descent from the Heveninghams whom she
regarded as 'one of the oldest families in England'.

She cherished a pedigree on an elaborate scroll about five feet long (now in
my possession), copied by some heraldic expert from an original in the
British Museum, which traces her family back in great detail to one 'Sir
Gualtir de Heveningham', complete with coat of arms, who is said to have
been living in 1020. As neither this type of name, nor the title, nor the art of
heraldry were current in England at this date 'Sir Gualtir' must be dismissed
as bogus and my brother, Charles Carrington, who made a careful study of
the Heveninghams would not accept any of them as fully authenticated
before Sir Philip who died in 1321. From him it was a straight run, vouched
for from other sources, to Elizabeth, the mother of Margaret, who used to
refer to her romantically as 'the last of the Heveninghams'. This was not
quite true. Descendants from branches further back do exist, mostly spelling
the name Henningham as it should also be pronounced.

The link with royalty is arrived at by side-stepping several times into the
female line and there is nothing unusual about it. Once you connect with
the higher nobility they are all intermarried—as much so as a group of
humble families in a country village—and you can establish a contact with
many of them in more ways than one. Ralph Nevill of Westmorland
(near the top of the page) had a huge family who married all the people most
worth marrying at that time, and he (like John of Gaunt) is an ancestor of
many sovereigns and tens of thousands of commoners.

The early Heveninghams also married into noble families bringing other
well-known people into our ancestry. Their coat of arms, shown overleaf,
was, in heraldic language, *quarterly or and gules, within a bordure engrailed
sable, charged with nine escallops argent. Crest, a Saracen's head.* In plainer words

EDWARD III = Philippa of Hainault
1312-77

John of Gaunt = (3) Catherine Swynford
1340-99   d.1403

Sir Ralph Nevill = (2) Lady Joan Beaufort
Earl of Westmoreland   d.1440

Richard Nevill
Earl of Salisbury 1400-69

John Nevill
Marquis of Montacute d.1471

Sir William Huddleston = Lady Isabel Nevill d.1516
of Sawston

Richard Huddleston d.1557

John Brooke = Lucy Huddleston fl. 1549
of Haselor
d. 1551

William Brooke of Haselor

William Brooke d. 1641

William Brooke d. 1672

Christopher Heveningham = Mary Brooke
d. 1737

Henry Heveningham 1693-1748

Charles Heveningham 1737-82

William Warner = Elizabeth Heveningham 1774-1823

Robert Parry = Margaret Warner 1806-1884

Heveningham
of Heveningham
in Suffolk

the simple quartering of gold and red was *differenced* in remote times by a black border of a special shape (*engrailed*), decorated with shells. These shells and the Saracen's head point clearly to a link with the Crusades.

This is a case where careful research proved an old pedigree to be reliable for most of its course, and provided links with other fascinating lines.

II

The Remoter Past

Going back into the past is like exploring a strange and remote land. For the first part of your journey the travelling is easy—wide roads, good signs, plenty of transport, but as you progress the amenities and aids are left behind one by one until at last you find yourself in the wilds with only the roughest kind of tracks, if any.

This is how it is when you reach the middle of the sixteenth century. Parish registers have ended; other parish records broke off a long way back; wills are scarcer; all records are scarce and those there are are harder to read. You have done extremely well to get so far and may be honourably excused if you decide to be content and go no further.

Or perhaps you have lost your way long before this. The trail may have ended for you in the seventeenth century or even sooner and you see no prospect of further progress. But if you are still keen to keep on, there are other tracks that you may be able to pick up with a bit of trouble. They are concerned chiefly with the ownership of land.

Before the eighteenth century nearly all wealth was in land. Those who made money bought houses and acres, thereby raising their social status as well as their incomes. Property involved lawyers and lawyers kept records, and the chief merit of records of this sort is that many of them cover such an immense period of time, some of them running without a break for seven centuries. Of course the richer your forbears were the more likely you are to find them in these legal records, but even a single farm with a few acres may be enough. You can at least try.

These records that I speak of are mostly among the Exchequer Records which are kept in the P.R.O. They may be seen in the Round Room—and, as at the British Museum Library, you have to have a seat to be able to order anything, so you are advised to be there early in the day.

Firstly there are the **Inquisitions Post Mortem** which were held to enquire exactly what a person owned at his death and to establish who his heir was, giving the relationship. They refer only to landowners of some importance, but as they have a typed index, giving name and county, you can soon see if the name you want is there. They run from 1235 to 1650.

Then there is a series called the **Feet of Fines** which is concerned with change of ownership by sale or gift. It gets its curious name from the fact that only the 'foot' of each document was preserved by the Exchequer, the rest being divided between the contracting parties. These pieces of parchment are hard to read, or so I have found, but mercifully brief, and useful because they often mention several members of the family.

But perhaps the most important series relating to property is the **Close Rolls** which records thousands of deeds of sale. They really are rolls, and of amazing length, each roll consisting of many deeds, each sewn on to the last as it was copied. As you unroll in one direction, seeking for the one you have ordered, you have to keep rolling up at the other end so as not to entangle your neighbours in yards of parchment. They would lend themselves well to slapstick comedy, but there is nothing like that in the Round Room. The atmosphere is thick with silent study.

The Feet of Fines and the Close Rolls both start about 1200 and continue right into the nineteenth century, so they may help you at many points, and needless to say the later ones are easier to read. You will of course begin with the indexes which are not difficult.

While you are in the Round Room, and perhaps waiting for some document you have ordered, you should study some of the other volumes on the shelves such as the printed calendars of the **Charter Rolls** or **Patent Rolls**. The difference between a calendar and an index is that the former gives a brief summary of the contents of each item. By using the indexes you can look through a number of volumes, dealing with a long period, and perhaps find some mention of the name that interests you.

Another set of records, that also come under the Exchequer but are not confined to the wealthy, are the **Lay Subsidies**. These are the returns of nationwide taxes levied at irregular intervals when the monarch was in special need of money. Only the very poor were exempted, and they show us a large number of ordinary householders in the parishes where they lived.

There is a useful one imposed by Henry VIII in 1524, and several of the time of Elizabeth I and James I, but these are less well preserved. But the ones that are the most valued by social historians are those that were laid on the unwilling people in the reigns of the three successive Edwards, I, II, and III, to pay for their wars against Scotland. Their dates, ranging from 1294 to 1332, make them by far the earliest lists of the majority of English house-holders by name, including mere cottagers. For the amateur genealogist they are almost too early. If you have your forbears established somewhere in the early Tudor period it is a long jump back to the early Edwards. Many events—such as the Black Death—had caused great movements of popula-tion during that time, and you can hardly expect your family to have remained in the same place. But it is exciting to look.

The originals of all these Subsidy Rolls can be seen in the Round Room, but a number of counties have had their section of the earliest ones printed, and these can also be seen elsewhere. A card index of P.R.O. records that are in print is available in the Waiting Room.

There remains still to be considered one more class of archives that sur-vive from medieval times in great numbers—**Manorial records**. They consist for the most part of Court Rolls (or at a later date Court Books), that is the minutes kept of the Manorial Courts, which were once the chief units of local administration, but which gradually through the centuries lost their powers to other authorities, such as the parish councils. However they continued to meet in villages throughout the country from Norman times to the nineteenth century and many of them have records that date from the fourteenth or even thirteenth century.

Many collections of manorial rolls are still in private hands; others have found their way into public repositaries. The staff at the County Record Office should know their whereabouts if they don't have them; or failing that it may possibly be worth writing to Quality House (see page 135), where the Manorial Documents Register is maintained by the Royal Commission on Historical Manuscripts.

Generally speaking, though not always, the Norman manor was the nucleus of the village and both continued with the same name, but a town or large village may have grown out of two or more manors, and some manors are called by the names of early owners. The local record office should be able to make this clear.

Being such ancient institutions manorial courts were great preservers of ancient customs and their doings are reported in a legal jargon from bygone times. But don't be alarmed by the strange expressions that you see, such as 'Court Baron and View of Frankpledge'; you can soon accustom yourself to the verbal oddities and find that in spite of their forbidding appearance they relate to quite ordinary human activities, concerned chiefly with farming and the land.

Whether or not you feel inspired to attack a large quantity of what may be difficult reading must depend on your own tastes and the time you can give to it, but if indeed the manorial rolls for the locality where your for-bears lived are easily available (a big if) then it would be a pity not to try.

A few words of guidance may make them more comprehensible. There is no need to read through all the formal headings and repetitions—what one might call rigmarole; as soon as you are familiar with the regular way in which it is all set out you can just pick out the personal names, and if one that interests you is there you can read that bit carefully.

You will find the date and the name of the Lord of the Manor in the elaborate heading which occupies the first three or four lines. As regards the date, see page 95 (and the whole of Chapter 12 for help with the reading). As to the Lord of the Manor you will get no more about him than his name, but by looking through a whole series you will see the succession of lords and the dates when they change.

After the heading you will see the word *Essoins* in the margin or, if the roll is in English 'Default of tenants'. This is a list of tenants of the manor who are fined a few pence each for not attending the court. As the majority did not attend unless they had special business to transact this is the likeliest place for you to see the name you want.

Immediately after that comes the *Homage*. This is the name given to a panel of local men—generally small farmers—who formed a sort of jury to report and adjudicate on local matters. They were sworn in with an oath of allegiance, or homage, to the lord.

Then come the complaints in detail which can be quite amusing. Some-body's pigs have gone astray; somebody's geese have spoilt the grass on the common; somebody's ditch has overflowed and flooded the lane; the ale in the tavern is not as it should be; and somebody's wife is a common scold.

There may be the annual appointments of the officials of the manor with a variety of traditional titles, the pindar, the ale conners, the tythingman and the headboroughs.

Finally comes the important business of registering change of ownership of manorial land. Someone selling a field or farm surrenders his rights in it and someone else is formally admitted. Or a death is reported and the heir established, and this may be accompanied by an extract from a will. This can be the very thing you want, but look first for the names and if they don't concern you skip it.

Not by any means did every landowner come under the jurisdiction of a manor. There were always freeholders and their numbers continually increased. But even they, if they farmed, were likely to own a few strips in the common fields, or to make use of grazing rights on the manorial wasteland. So most of the residents of the neighbourhood do appear from time to time in these court rolls.

Among the rolls you may occasionally find a *rental*, which is a list of all the tenants at that date and what they had to pay—very useful. And if you see one of your forbears put down for a minute sum you needn't assume he was a poor cottager. He might be just that, but he could also have a large property with only a small bit of it owing manorial rents.

Unfortunately manorial records were written in Latin until the middle of the eighteenth century, with the exception of the Commonwealth period when it was ruled that they should be kept in English. It seems incredibly stupid that they reverted to Latin after that, especially when you consider what a typically English institution the manor was and how rustic its character. However the Latin that is used is a very simple unclassical sort that lapses into English when the clerk is stuck for a word, and the personal names at least remain recognizable. My advice to the beginner who is not a Latin scholar is to start by looking at some of the later records, that were kept in English, or those of the 1650s, so as to become familiar with the style and arrangement, and then when you attempt some Latin ones you will find that you can make out pretty well what is going on. If you find a bit that you particularly want to read correctly there will probably be someone at hand to help you. Plates 6 and 7 show examples.

Summing up manorial records—they might give you a lot of help as well as picturesque background material, but it is uncertain if you can find the right ones, and if you can there will be no indexes to help you. You will be dependant on your own industry. The experience should make you more appreciative of the vast amount of work that has gone into the indexing of so many of our national records.

All the records mentioned in this chapter have the possibility of helping you at widely differing periods, and of taking you back to the earliest times you are at all likely to penetrate. Few people succeed in tracing their families much before 1500 unless they get on to one of those ready-made pedigrees, but if your name is unusual, or if your people can be identified by always owning the same piece of land, you may at least catch glimpses of them from time to time throughout the Middle Ages.

Reading Old Documents

The reading of old manuscripts may present a problem but not unless they are really old. Back to 1700 one should find no difficulty but in the century before, especially in its first quarter, the situation is very different. The reigns of the later Tudors and early Stewarts were a time of great change in writing as in other matters and much variation may be met with in manuscripts written at about the same date.

To understand the state of affairs we must go back a little further. All through the Middle Ages English clerks kept their records in a fairly neat traditional script that is sometimes called *Gothic*. Its chief fault was that too many small letters looked too much alike, especially i, m, n, u and v, which when packed close together were impossible to distinguish. Added to this c was only slightly curved if at all and very like t which was often no taller. Examples of three words written in Gothic-style small letters are given below. As if to counteract the sameness of the small letters the capitals were apt to be elaborate, and, to us, unexpected.

Many contractions were used by the clerks of the Middle Ages, which means that letters were omitted, this being indicated by a mark above the word. It was mostly in Latin, and was in fact a business for specialists.

monumentum

interdictum

minimum

Among professional writers none were more important than the lawyers especially those of the higher courts. Gradually they developed their own set styles of writing, the clerks of the Exchequer specializing in one set of loops and flourishes while those of Chancery preferred another. These legal styles, offshoots of the old Gothic tradition, are known as **Court hands.** At first sight they look baffling, especially some of the capitals, illustrated on this page.

About the end of the fifteenth century a new style of writing came into England from Italy. It was just in time to be adopted for the new art of printing which was then in its infancy and this was fortunate for it was a great improvement both in clarity and elegance on the old script. It was also used for formal inscriptions, as for instance on tombs and monuments where it was particularly appropriate, for the new styles in architecture fashionable at that time were also the product of Renaissance Italy. Our modern writing, whether printed or by hand, derives directly from this style.

We now use the terms 'Roman' or 'Italic' to distinguish our two main kinds of type in use, but in Tudor England either word could be applied to the **Italian style.** 'We think we do know the sweet Roman hand' said Malvolio of Olivia's letter, implying that she wrote in the new exclusive mode. But few people wrote so at that time. Shakespeare himself, judging by his signature, was very much of the old school.

For although all educated men of that time must have read the new style of lettering with ease, very few of them wrote that way, and actually more were writing than ever before. One of the many changes that took place in Tudor England was the great increase in literacy. By Elizabeth's reign it was normal for all gentlemen and business men to write fluently, which was far from the case a century

𝒜	𝒜	A
ℬ	ℬ	B
¢	φ	C
∂	∮	D
€	€	E
∫	∬	F
∮	𝒢	G
ℏ	ℋ	H
∫	I and J	
ƙ	β	K
𝓛	𝓛	L
ℳ	𝓂	M
𝓃	𝓅	N
∅	φ	O
𝒫	𝒫	P
𝒬	𝒬	Q

before. They had learned the art in the grammar schools or with private tutors trained in the old ways and they wrote in a hand known as **Secretary**, an informal, cursive style that had, like the Court hands of the lawyers, grown out of the old Gothic script. Despite its clarity and crispness, the Italian style was to win no easy victory over this vigorous English growth.

So we have the anomaly that you may read the inscription on an Elizabethan tomb with perfect ease but if the will of the man buried there was in your hand, or the register recording his death, you might find it hard to make out more than a few words.

By the end of Charles I's reign Secretary hand had lost the battle against Italic (both Charles and Cromwell wrote very modern hands) but far into the second half of that century there were plenty of old gentlemen writing in the manner they had learned as boys, while lawyers—always great conservers of past customs—clung to their own special mannerisms which you may well encounter as you try to read a seventeenth-century will, even a late one.

In parish registers the change often comes suddenly. The old parson in—say—the 1630s or 1640s writes as he has always done, his letters growing more shaky every year, until his burial is recorded by his successor, fresh from the university, in a beautiful Italian script that looks quite modern to our eyes.

At the first glance Secretary looks difficult. Like all cursive hands it varies greatly with the writer and the occasion. Informal notes, hastily written, can be terrible. But most parsons took some trouble with their registers; wills were neatly copied by lawyers' clerks trained to write with precision and consistency, and only a few of the letters are totally different from our own.

The Secretary capital letters, which are given on these two pages, are rather more different than the small letters. They were used more lavishly than we use them—not only for proper nouns but for any word that the writer felt was important in the sentence.

Take special note of C with its horizontal stroke, and try not to confuse the other more modern-looking C with T.

In Secretary hand capital F consists of two small fs which explains why some people still spell their surnames in that way. You might mistake it for a capital H, but only if you were very inexperienced for the old H is not like that at all.

Another important thing to remember is that there was no difference between Secretary I and J. The same letter served for both and this was also the case with Secretary U and V.

The small letters—illustrated here and overleaf—are more like our own but a few of them need to be specially learned: notably c, which to us looks quite unfamiliar, like a modern r (see Plate 5).

Little e needs careful watching too. It has an extra kink in it and can be mistaken for an o. This e lasted a long time and can sometimes appear right down to 1800 in hands that otherwise look quite modern.

Another letter which disguises the appearance of many words is h; it had a huge tail looping down and up again below the line, and often influencing its next neighbour. The article 'the', being written so often, could assume a simplified form which has been mistaken for 'ye' and still lives on in a spurious vitality over the door of many a 'Ye olde shoppe'.

Another unexpected letter is r. In all periods it has had variable forms. In the older script it came down below the line (see page 88), or alternatively it could look like a small z, a form which may appear up to about 1600. But in most Secretary hands it looks like a neat little w. Even now we have two quite different ways of forming r in our handwriting.

John the sonne of Richard Curtis
and Alice his wife. bap. x Maye

But the old-fashioned letter that probably stayed longest was the long s that looks like an f (except that it is not crossed half way up). It was never used to end words. The final s was often just a little twiddle with an upward flourish.

If you are faced with a document in a difficult hand the best way to tackle it is to make your own alphabet from it. The letters illustrated on pages 90–92 should help you, but don't copy them; copy those you can identify from the document. Every writer has his own idiosyncrasies and there may be some letters—especially capitals—formed in an unusual style. There is bound to be something that you can read. If you have ordered the manuscript from an index you know what you have ordered and the name of at least one person and one place that you can recognise should be near the heading. If it is an early Will it will begin in the standard way (page 34). That will give you several capital letters and many more small ones and the act of copying them carefully will fix them in your mind so that you will know them again.

With parish registers you know in advance the kind of information that will be given, and the regular statements about baptisms, marriages and deaths will soon be recognizable. The important items are the names, and the Christian names will be the easiest to start with. It is certain that John, William, Richard, Thomas, Mary, Elizabeth and Ann will appear over and over again. Make your alphabet from them and any other words you are sure of, and when you come to the surnames don't guess from the general effect but look at each letter critically, and you will soon find it getting easier.

Reading an unfamiliar hand is like speaking a foreign language. The best way to learn it is to plunge in and do it.

There is a useful book on old handwriting by F. G. Emmison (page 118).

The prospect of being faced with Latin may cause some apprehension, but you can go a long way before you meet it. Wills are always in English, and so are the majority of parish registers right from their Tudor beginnings, although vicars were always inclined to scatter a few Latin headings about the page, most of them like *Anno Domini*, *Baptismae* and *Matrimoniae* requiring no translation.

For registers entirely in Latin you will need to master only a few words and most of these could easily be guessed. Here is a very short glossary, including abbreviations that might be used.

nupti sunt, nupt'	were married
sepultus est, sepult'	was buried
et uxor eijus, et ux' eius	and his wife
vidua, vid'	widow
filius, fils	son
filia	daughter
miles, mil'	knight
armiger, arm'	one entitled to bear arms
generosus, gen'	gentleman (similar to above)
infans	baby
puer, puella	boy child, girl child
soluta	spinster

Apart from these phrases, the Roman numerals, and the names of the months, you should need little more for a register unless the vicar launches into some extra comment.

With legal deeds and manorial Court Rolls in Latin the vocabulary needed is again limited and can be learned, but it is much wider than what you find in a register, less human, less familiar and altogether more difficult. It would not be so bad—one could struggle on with the aid of a dictionary—if it were not for all the abbreviations or contractions that make words unrecognisable. Before the invention of printing, when everything, including whole books, was written by hand, more and more short cuts were evolved. The abbreviated forms shown above are simple; they consist only of omitting the last few letters and replacing them with a small upward flourish of the pen (shown here as an apostrophe). But contractions were also made by omitting letters from the middle of a word, which was shown by a line or wiggle above it. There was a special tendency to omit n and m so that a word like *omnia* (everything) could be written *oīa*.

If you have some Latin manorial records available, and are keen to try and read them, the standard book to help you is C. T. Martin's *Record Interpreter* of which every record office has a copy. It gives a long list of all the regular contractions that you are likely to meet, and a glossary of the Latin words that are found in medieval records but not in classical Latin. But it assumes you know that. A simpler book for beginners is Eileen Gooder's *Latin for Local History*. One encouraging point is that both surnames and place-names are generally written out in full and you can at least recognise those.

Apart from the regular omissions of letters there were a number of special signs for short words or syllables that occurred frequently. The most important of these are the signs for *per, pre* and *pro*, all consisting of the letter p with some additional mark on it, as illustrated below. I call them important because they were very firmly rooted and lasted a long time. When the writing of English became common in the Tudor period, together with the advent of printed books, the habit of contracting words fortunately dwindled, but the sign for *per* was very persistent and was used by all writers of Secretary hand. In the spelling of those days little distinction was made between 'er' and 'ar' ('person' and 'parson' are the same in origin) and so this same sign was used equally for 'par'. A word in which you may see it very often is 'parishe' which when contracted looks like 'pishe'.

℞ *per* or *par*   ℘ *pro*   p̄ *pre*

𝓉𝒽𝑒 𝓅𝒾𝓈𝒽𝑒   *the parishe*

As regards writing, the old English script is no harder to read than the Tudor hands. In fact it is easier, or would be if it were not for the Latin and the contractions. You may see examples of it on pre-Reformation tombs in churches, where the inscription often begins *Orate pro anima*—('Pray for the soul of—') But what it looks like is:

Ọrate p aīa

After the Reformation praying for souls was frowned on and inscriptions on tombs began instead *Hic jacet*—('Here lies—').

In Latin documents such as manorial rolls Christian names are generally given in latinised forms and then contracted too, but they always begin in the familiar way and are not hard to recognize. The commonest ones are the most likely to be contracted: John in Latin is *Johannes* and is written *Johēs*; William becomes *Willelmus* and then *Willūs*; Richard is *Ricardus* and so *Ricūs*. Unusual names are written in full and surnames are seldom tampered with (not after about 1400). If a parish register was kept in Latin you will get the same thing there, but it is not a serious problem so long as you understand the general principle. Just remember when you see the girl babies being christened—apparently—*Johanna* and *Margareta* that they are really only Joan and Margaret.

One more point should be mentioned in connection with old documents, the way in which they are dated. In manorial and other legal deeds it was generally the custom to date by the regnal year of the sovereign. Thus instead of saying 'on the thirtieth day of April, 1510' they say 'the thirtieth daye of April in the second yeare of the raigne of our Soveraine Lord Henrie viii by the Grace of God,' etc. Henry became king on April 22, 1509. So to get a date quite accurate you need to know not only the year but also the day and month when each sovereign acceded. But any record office will have a list of regnal years, or there is one in Richardson's *Local Historian's Encyclopedia*.

Finally it should be remembered that until 1752 New Year's day was on March 25. Thus in old registers January, February and most of March follow on under the same date as the preceding December. After the revised calendar came into use you may find marginal notes by the vicar about Old Style or New Style. He may be a bit muddled about it but there is no need for you to be so.

The majority of English surnames come to us from the Middle Ages, some from as far back as the Conquest. They are in fact our oldest personal possessions. Unfortunately they don't tell us very much about our forbears, but they do constitute our main lifeline back into the past, and anyone who cares about his ancestors must also feel a strong interest in the name he has inherited from them.

Some of the most intriguing surnames—those that come from personal nicknames—are the least help genealogically (unless of course they are rare— a rare name always helps), but even they can establish the race of the man described. It will not advance your search to know that a remote ancestor was extremely fair—White, Swan, Snow, Lilywhite—or exceptionally dark— Black, Dunn, Raven, Crowe—but at least you know that he was English. Among the Normans he would have been Blunt, Blunden, or Blundell (all related to the French *blond*), or perhaps Corbin or Corbett, both meaning 'little crow'. Again the Saxons might call a tall man a Crane (a long-legged bird now extinct in England). The Normans used exactly the same simile, and the Old French word *grue* survives as the surname Grew. Some others that are derived from Norman nicknames are Russell (red-haired), Curtis (courteous), Bassett (short), Beale (handsome) and Lovatt or Lovell (young wolf). Pettigrew means 'with feet like a crane', Pettifer 'with feet of iron'. But the great majority are English.

Surnames fall roughly into four types: **nicknames**, which include many of the oldest; **patronymics**, which give the name of a parent; those that tell of **occupation** or **status**; and those that give the **place of origin**. This last group is the most useful in tracing ancestry.

In Chapter 1 something was said of the surnames that consist of place-names that can be pin-pointed on the map. From the genealogical point of view this is the best sort to have, for, apart from the interest of the local origin, they are generally in themselves unusual. Place-names have an infinite variety, and although many of them with simple meanings, such as Newton (new farm), are repeated in many areas, yet a vast number of them are unique.

Most people whose surnames are names of villages like to assume that their ancestors were lords of the manors of those places, and this must often have been the case. In the period following the Conquest when surnames were beginning to stick like tags, it was very usual for landowners to be named from their places of abode in this way. But the truth must be told that the same name could also become attached quite as naturally to humble people who moved away from their native villages to seek work elsewhere and were known by the names of the places they had come from. The surnames of apprentice boys in London as seen in thirteenth century records include village names from all over England.

However a great many families did continue to live in the neighbourhood where the name belonged and are still to be found not too far distant, and the smaller the village the more likely it is that they acquired the name by being its principal family. The converse is certainly true; if your name is that of a large town—large long ago—like York, or Lincoln, or Bristol, your family obviously didn't own the place; they merely came from there like many others. Incidentally an old form of Bristol was Bristow, and that is how it remains as a surname.

It often happens that a surname can be recognized as a place-name and yet not found in any gazetteer. This is because thousands of place-names have never been known beyond their own localities. In former times when people's lives were more closely bound up with the land they had a name for every patch of ground, every hillock or hollow, every clump of trees and certainly every inhabited spot. Some of these have become the names of towns and cities; some are still known only locally; some are totally forgotten but may yet live on as surnames for families whose forbears once lived in those places.

You can tell that a surname originated as a place-name if it ends with one of the regular place-name elements such as -hill, -ford, -wood, -brook, -well, and so on. These are easily understood; others of the same sort which were also common nouns of locality once but are now less easily recognised are -ton, -ham, -stead, -worth, and -wick which all meant a farm or small settlement. Other common local endings are -ley or -leigh (a clearing), -don (a hill), and -bury (a fortified place); and there are a great many more. If your surname ends in one of these ways it almost certainly began as a place-name, but it may be anywhere in the country for these elements are all widespread. The only way you could locate it, if it is not in that gazetteer, is by going through the indexes of the English Place-Name Society volumes. These are detailed studies of the names of each county and contain far more names than can be found in print elsewhere, but unfortunately only about half the counties have been covered so far.

Some place-name endings can be distinguished as belonging to particular parts of the country and these can give a general indication as to where the family came from. For instance, the Danes who settled in the northern part of England just before the Conquest had many distinctive words that are common in place-names there but never found in the south. Chief among them is the ending -by, meaning a farm. Other unmistakable Danish elements are *thorpe* (a village), *thwaite* (a clearing), *holm* (a flat-topped island) and *garth* (an enclosure). If one of these makes part or the whole of your surname your forbears came from a northern region.

Some surnames reflect the southern or the northern form of the same word: Church and Kirk, Bridge and Brigg, Long and Lang. The second of each of these pairs would come from northern England or Scotland. Dale belongs to the north while Coombe (or Coombes or the ending -combe) is typical of the south-west. Both are words for valleys.

Cornish place-names have a decided character of their own being mostly formed in the old Cornish language. As in all the Celtic tongues the noun normally comes first with descriptive words following (the opposite of the English order), and so it is the beginnings of names that are the most distinctive. Tre- (a farm), Pol- (a harbour) and Pen- (a headland) are among the commonest. When Cornish families began to use surnames they were nearly all taken from the names of their farms and they are easily recognisable. There are places in Wales too that begin with Tre-, Pol-, and Pen- but the Welsh, strangely enough, have hardly any surnames of local origin.

Some surnames tell plainly the district from which your family came: Kent, Hampshire, Wilsher, Dossett (never mind the spelling), but it must be realized that it was long, long ago that they left those places, for people received such surnames only when they had moved somewhere else, and that at a time when surnames were still in the making. A man might be known by the name of a village while continuing to live in it, if he was its leading inhabitant, but it would be no distinction to call him by the name of the county he lived in. A Cornishman who stayed in Cornwall until surnames were fully established would have one like Trevelyan or Penruddick. But if he migrated into England before that time he might receive the tag of Cornwall (often spelt Cornwell or Cornell), Cornish or Cornwallis, or perhaps Curno, as he would have said it in his own language.

However, many Cornishmen came no further than Devon; many who became known as Welsh (or Welch) settled in Cheshire, Shropshire or other western counties; the Scotts were once mostly found in the border country (though they have since spread everywhere). And to look at the other side of the coin, the surnames English and England originated not in England but among her neighbours. Inglis is the Scottish form of 'English'.

Then there are racial names from further afield given in England so long ago that, though they tell of a foreign origin, they are themselves thoroughly English: Dane, Norman, French, Flemming; Brett, Brittain, Britton (all from Brittany); Gascoigne and Gaskin (from Gascony) and others. We all know when the Danes and Normans came upon us and the Flemings and Bretons were not far behind for William the Conqueror had help from both of them in his invasion and encouraged them to share in the spoils. Incidentally 'French' seems to have been the word most often used for the Normans at that time, and in many cases the name Francis has this same origin. In medieval records you often see *le franceys* meaning 'the Frenchman' and as the word acclimatized it developed in these two ways. These racial names have been English for anything up to nine hundred years.

Of course the Normans brought some of their own surnames with them and coined others in their own language after they were here, as already illustrated earlier in this chapter. Many of them called themselves after the places they had come from in Normandy and at least three hundred English family names have been identified with Norman villages. The most typical element of Norman village names is the ending -*ville*, which we see in such surnames as Nevill, Grenville, Melville and so on. But names of this type are extremely varied and their spelling has often suffered strange changes. As they were at first the names of the ruling class the heads of families took pride in preserving a semblance of their French form, but as younger sons and their descendants became gradually assimilated to the ordinary English people around them, their surnames took on a more English character. Thus descendants of the Grenvilles can also be Grenfell or Greenfield; Beauchamp could be written Beecham; Sommerville could turn into Summerfield; and Mowbray into Mumbray or Mummery. In fact more surnames are of Norman origin than you might expect.

These and other continental surnames absorbed into England in the Middle Ages are a totally different matter from foreign ones brought in in more modern times, most of which have preserved an alien character by which they may be recognized. The last big influx of French names of which many were anglicized are those of the Huguenots, who came as the result of religious persecution in 1685. If you have reason to believe that your family may have been among them you can enquire about their records from the Huguenot Society (page 134).

Another class of surnames now intermingled with English names everywhere and yet clearly distinguishable from them in origin are those of the neighbouring Celtic countries. Those of Scotland and Ireland are too numerous and too well-known to be discussed here but you may look them up in detail in books given on pages 117 and 119 under the authors Black and MacLysaght. However it is useful to remember that before the mid-eighteenth century the diverse inhabitants of the British Isles were far more tidily contained within their own territories than they are now. Though a good many Lowland Scots came into England after the union of the crowns in 1603 the famous clan names of the Highlands were rarities south of the Border until the troubles following the disastrous rising of 1745 which dispersed them, not only into England, but round the world. Again there are few Irish surnames to be found among English records before 1800 except in the western counties.

The Welsh, on the other hand, have been overflowing freely into England since the thirteenth century and particularly so since the Welsh Tudors came to the throne. (All the same the movement in both directions has accelerated in the last century.) There are many families in England with Welsh surnames but with no tradition of a Welsh origin because it is so remote. In their own homeland the Welsh were very late in adopting fixed surnames and until about 1600 were still using patronymics that changed with each generation, the son of Evan ap Hugh becoming Owen ap Evan, and his son (perhaps another Hugh) being called Hugh ap Owen. But any of them who settled in England conformed to the English habit and stuck to the name then in use without further change.

Unlike their cousins the Cornish, whose surnames are almost all local, the Welsh nearly always used patronymics and this resulted in an acute lack of variety, especially as—at the time they adopted fixed surnames—they had also adopted in a big way the very Christian names that were most popular in England. Jones (son of John) may be recognized as Welsh in origin by its spelling and pronunciation (as compared with the English Johns or Johnson); Davies also is almost exclusively Welsh; but Williams, Hughes, Roberts and Edwards can also be English although it is the Welsh who have given them their large numbers. Actually the English, who acquired fixed surnames two or three centuries before the Welsh, did so in a much more natural and colloquial manner, and the majority of their patronymics are formed from the familiar abbreviations used in conversation. Thus the son of William most probably became Wills, Wilson, Wilkins, Wilkes, Willett, or one of several other popular forms. Robert was generally turned into Robin and from that familiar name came many surnames ranging from Robinson and Robson, to the rhymed Hobbs and Dobbs; while the commonest surname derived from John in England was Jackson. On the whole the full-length William and Robert, each with the addition of 's' are generally Welsh, just as Williamson and Robertson are probably Scottish. The Scots, like the English, have a great variety of surnames, some very old, but in the time of the troubles when many clansmen were obliged to change their names they often made one in this way from their father's name.

But the Welsh have also their own distinctive patronymics formed from their true Welsh personal names such as Griffiths, Meredith, Llewelyn, Rhys, Morgan, Evan and Owen. A few old Welsh nicknames have also survived, such as the surnames Lloyd (grey), Gwynn (white), Gough (red), and Vaughan (little). Another distinctively Welsh group are those that preserve the 'p' from *ap* (meaning 'son of'—). Prichard, Parry, Pugh, Price and Powell are the sons of Richard, Harry, Hugh, Rhys and Hywel. When *ap* was followed by a vowel the 'p' changed to 'b', hence Bowen and Bevan. None of these surnames can be anything but Welsh.

The surname Lewis can occasionally come from the French Louis, but this was never much used in England. In the great majority of cases Lewis is 'the son of Llewi', a shortened form of Llewelyn.

The surnames that arose from occupation and status are seldom helpful in locating a family, as similar conditions and needs produced the same ones in all parts of the country, but none the less they are full of interest. The names that are commonest are not those of the most numerous workers but of the men who had skills that made them pre-eminent, each in his own district, the Smith on whom all depended for tools and weapons, the Wright who built in timber, the Webster (or weaver as we would say now), the Turner who fashioned cups and bowls on his lathe, and many others.

The tendency, sometimes heard, to decry these names from trades as being plebeian is very foolish. Masters of their crafts, these men had already risen above the masses of the peasants who tilled the soil for their manorial lords. At a time when the great majority were still in partial bondage they were free. A Smith or a Miller in (say) 1300 could save enough to buy himself land where his descendants would be yeomen and perhaps gentry in a few generations. Incidentally the surnames Freeman and Franklin (which have the same meaning) stress the point that it was a great distinction to be free.

In these occupational surnames we see the typical figures of the medieval world, the Hunter, the Fisher, the Fowler, and the Woodman of the forests; the Knights, Squires and Archers who set out on the Crusades, and the Palmers who followed in their wake as pilgrims and came back with pieces of palm to show they had reached the Holy Land. We see the households of the rich, each with its Butler, Page and Chamberlain (or more familiarly Chambers) who looked after the sleeping quarters, the Spencer who dispensed the stores, the Falconer (or Faulkner) who tended the much-prized hawks, the Harper who provided entertainment, and many more.

The church is represented in strength; but here we must be wary; the Bishops, Abbotts and Priors are not to be taken at their face value. The working man in England has always enjoyed his joke and in the Middle Ages nicknames were coined as freely from prominent people as from birds and beasts. If a man was vain of his appearance he might be dubbed 'the Peacock'; if he was pompous he might become the 'Bishop'. Even the Pope could be called into play. There were no real popes in England but there were plenty of people inclined to lay down the law and Pope became a regular nickname.

However, surnames derived from the humbler ranks of the clergy generally spring from truth. Each village had its priest and if the clergy had not been officially celibate Parson would probably have been as common a name as Smith. Even so there are a fair number but nearly all with a final s, which is not usual with names of occupation. It implies that the surname did not generally originate with the parson himself but with someone connected with him, a relative or servant. In the fourteenth-century Subsidy Rolls (page 84) we can see such names in their original forms, as for instance 'Simon atte persones' (at the parson's) or 'Henry Parsoncosyn' (the parson's cousin).

But the modern surname that represents the medieval church—or rather its teaching—in the largest numbers is Clark. In later times when a man is described in a legal document as a clerk or *clericus* it generally means that he was a priest, but in the period when surnames were being formed it was the ordinary colloquial use of the word that made the name. And its normal meaning in conversation was a man who could read and write. It was used for lawyers, secretaries, students, the intellectuals in an illiterate age. Every landowner needed a clerk to manage his affairs, and the surname is a common one because, like Smith, it represents a great service to the community; but that is little consolation to those who want to trace their ancestors and find Clarks on every side.

In modern times the problem of too many people with the same name has been solved for many families by the use of double surnames, with or without hyphens. But this was a nineteenth-century development, which is not likely to help you for more than three or four generations. However it is in itself a pointer to another line of ancestry, and perhaps one that will be easier to follow.

Nor will an unusual spelling be any use in guiding you far on your quest. I have heard people say 'Oh, but our family have always spelt it with an e.' But once you are back into the eighteenth century, an e here or there is as nothing, and you must expect to meet your name in every kind of spelling, but generally more or less phonetic. Actually the commoner names have an advantage here, and are rather more consistently spelt than unusual ones which can be strangely distorted. But never reject a surname as not being one of yours because it is not spelt as you think it should be.

The best hope for tracing a family with a common name is that its members lived in a small community and stayed there, preferably owning land. It is also a great help if they used uncommon Christian names—of which more in the next chapter.

This is a very brief glance at a large subject. If you want to read more about it see page 119. The best dictionary of surnames is by P. H. Reaney, but no dictionary can possibly include them all or has yet attempted to do so, for they run into tens of thousands and the same one (in origin) has often taken half a dozen different forms. Dr Reaney chose to omit most of those that consist of English place-names, so if you don't find yours remember to look in a gazetteer as well, but he did include most of those that come from Norman place-names as they would be much harder for anyone but an expert to identify.

If you look up your name in this dictionary be sure to squeeze all the significance you can out of the few facts given beyond the bare meaning. The language from which it comes will give a hint of background. If it is Old French (O.F.) the surname probably developed among the Normans, or if Scandinavian (O Da or ON) you can conclude that you have Viking blood.

The majority of origins will be Old English (OE) and among these you can often find an indication of their antiquity as surnames. Most Old English words are still current in the modern language though their form may have changed somewhat, but others have been obsolete for many centuries and survive only as surnames: Snell, for example, meant quick and bold, Kemp a warrior, Unwin, a stranger. Such personal descriptions could only have been acquired when the words were still in common use not long after the Conquest.

Again a great many patronymics can be dated by their linguistic character. Christian names that were brought in by the Normans (William, Robert, Richard, etc.) have been popular ever since and surnames have been formed from them over a long period, but many personal names of a much earlier vintage still exist among our surnames. Aylwin and Aylward are the Saxon *Aethelwin* and *Aethelward*; Goodrich and Goodrick both come from *Godric* a favourite Saxon name; Loveridge and Leveridge come from *Leofric*, Livesy from *Leofsig*, and Wolsey from *Wulfsig*. These are just a few out of hundreds that come to us straight from the Anglo-Saxons. The Normans never took to them and they dropped out of use with surprising rapidity, surviving only as surnames. Being unfamiliar they have been much contracted and eroded by time and are not easy to recognize except for experts in this field, but if you look up your surname and find it is an Old English personal name (the capital letter will show that it is a proper name and not a descriptive nickname) you will know that you come of genuine old English stock.

One more clue that the surname dictionary may give you relates to locality. For each entry a few of the earliest known examples of the name are given with their sources and county of origin, shown in abbreviated form. If the name is unusual these sources are worth noting. They may all come from one district, and at least they indicate where the name existed at an early date.

What we need is a dictionary of surnames that would specialize in giving the natural habitat of each name. An attempt to cover the distribution of English surnames in his own time was made in 1890 by H. B. Guppy (see page 118) but the task was too large for him and he wasted too much energy in trying to give proportionate numbers of common surnames in each county. I have found his book disappointing, but for others it might have something useful.

A much more important undertaking is the *English Surnames Series* which is setting out to deal with the history and distribution of surnames in each county. The work goes forward and will be invaluable.

In the process of tracing ancestors one is generally hunting for a particular surname, but there are times when Christian names can be nearly as important, and the disadvantage of a too common surname can be much mitigated by unusual first names, especially if repeated in several generations. It is fortunate for all those engaged in family history that a strong feeling persisted for centuries in favour of calling children after their parents, grandparents, and other relations, as if to bind the family together by that means as well as by the surname. This fashion has almost gone now due to the modern habit of using Christian names so freely. The change has come rapidly—among so many other changes of our time—and young people of today hardly realize that in the early part of this century the Christian names of adults were seldom heard outside the small home circle. Even there the names of aunts and uncles were politely prefixed with the relationship—Aunt Lucy, Uncle Alec—parents were Mother and Father to the children and often to each other, and Mr and Mrs So-and-So to almost everyone else. Men who were close friends would drop the 'Mr' and use the surname only, perhaps in a shortened or jocular form, but Christian names remained very private. But now when adults are Peter, Mike and Jane to everyone, they look for something different for their children. The possibilities too have widened and the choice is enormous.

During the whole period in which you are most likely to be ancestor-hunting —say from 1600 to 1900—it was normal practice to call the first son after his father or one of his grandfathers unless there was a very special reason why some other person was to be propitiated. Second and third sons were generally given family names too and it was only then that parents could let their fancies wander to something more original. As families were large new names, and often 'fashionable' ones, did appear for younger children.

Of course a great many of the children died (in the eighteenth century the mortality of children in their first year was in the region of 50%) and so chance took a hand in deciding which names survived and the regular repetition is not so apparent as it might have been. But in some families a father was so anxious to have a son of his exact name to succeed him that if little Thomas failed to survive the next boy was called Thomas again, and the parish burial register may show a succession of little brothers called Thomas. It sometimes even happened that if a child was sickly the same wished-for name was given to the next one just to be sure of it—and this at a time when one Christian name was the normal thing. Two brothers of the same name is unthinkable today, but searchers among old records should be warned that they may come across it. I remember being very confused with the owner of some land in Hoddesdon in about 1600 who seemed to have two wives at the same time, until I read in his father's will that the land was to be divided between 'my son William Sharnbrooke the elder and my son William Sharnbrooke the younger'. They must have had different names for family use, but legal documents don't tell you that sort of thing.

The tendency to repeat family names (if not carried to excess) is a boon to genealogists, though not so much in the case of very common names, and a small number has been immensely popular for a very long time. The Anglo-Saxons, having no surnames, used an enormous variety of personal names, hundreds of them, and mostly now forgotten. As mentioned in the last chapter, the Normans brought in a completely new fashion, consisting firstly of the Frankish names of their own royal family led by William, Richard, Robert and Henry, and then of Biblical names, which the Saxons had never used, and of which the best loved was John. By about a century after the Conquest these names were established favourites throughout the country, and they have held that position unshakably ever since.

All that time, about seven centuries, John has been the most popular man's name in England. William has run it very close and in the sixteenth century was for a time almost ahead, but in recent years it has fallen behind, though it seems now on the way back. Thomas, boosted in public esteem by the murder and canonization of Becket, has probably been third favourite, with Richard, Robert and Henry never far off. For girls the picture has been less clear cut, with fashion playing a stronger part, but since about 1600 Mary, Elizabeth, Jane and Anne have always been in the forefront with Katherine, Sarah and Margaret in support. And all the time there has been a delightful variety of rarer names, the ones that genealogists like best.

So if you are working on a family with a rather common surname—say Cooper for instance—neither John nor William as first names will be much help with identification. Supposing you are looking for the birth of John Cooper over a fairly wide area and you find one of about the right date in a parish register; the doubts must arise, is he the right one? Now is the time when the importance of noting all the children of each generation comes into its own. Your original John Cooper, the one you know about, had sons named John, Robert, and Nathaniel, and daughters, Mary, Jane and Rebecca. The one whose birth you have just found is the son of Robert and Mary Cooper. So far so good. But read on. Did they have other children? If they had a Nathaniel or a Rebecca or better still both you will know you have got your man. The moral is—always record every name you find in the family you are studying, even those of children who lived only a few days. Single Christian names can be good evidence, if not too common, but a whole pattern of names can be conclusive.

The drawback to the regular repetition of names is that you may often find that several brothers have all dutifully called a son after their father, with the result that cousins have identical names, and if this goes on even a rare combination of names (rare as regards the whole country) can be met several times over in one area. This can be tiresome, but at least you know they are related.

It is not until the eighteenth century that one begins to find more than one name being given to a child at christening and this remains very much the exception until well into the Victorian age. When you do meet them they are an enormous help with identification, often making all the difference between doubt and certainty.

When the second name is a surname you have special cause to be grateful. Not only do you get a much rarer combination but probably also a clue to another line of ancestry. But don't rely on that. Samuel Taylor Coleridge, for example, the youngest of a large family, was named after a Mr Samuel Taylor who lived nearby and was his godfather, though apparently no real relation. Friends and connections honoured in this marked way were generally godparents.

But more often a surname added like this does lead to a direct line of descent although it may be some way back. I think for example of my father's grandfather, Henry Incledon Johns. We knew he was born in Cornwall and the names of his parents, but his mother's name was not Incledon and there the matter rested for a time. Then I discovered Boyd's Marriage Index in the

Genealogists' library, and looking through the volumes for Cornwall was soon able to identify the village of St Keverne as the main hub of Incledons. When at last I had its registers before me I found the ramifications of a large family, linking neatly with H. I. Johns and leading back delightfully into the past. He had been named after his great-uncle, Henry Incledon, whose will dated 1792 left a small legacy to his young kinsman and namesake.

In my experience most early occurrences of double baptismal names in which the second one is a surname were, like these examples, tributes to particular people whose complete names were given to make the compliments unmistakable. In the case just mentioned it wasn't enough to name the boy Henry. He may have had other relations of that name and there must be no doubt whom the tribute was aimed at. I am glad they were so specific. Henry got his legacy and I a whole range of ancestors whom I might never have located if he had been only Henry Johns.

One more example will show both how unexpected and how useful these double names can be. The direct ancestry of my father's other grandfather, Nicholas Toms Carrington (see page 52), has always been something of a mystery and several of my family have worked at it over the years. We used to think that Toms was his mother's maiden name, but it proved to be not so. Then at last I found the marriage of his widowed grandmother, Barbary Carrington, to Nicholas Toms, an attorney of Plymouth Dock. So our great-grandfather, N.T.C., had been called after his step-grandfather, to whom we have no relationship.

The discovery of this second marriage was significant in several ways—as mentioned on page 51—not least that it bound those three generations together without a doubt. It also raised some points of human interest. Barbary's boy, Henry, was twelve when she remarried and soon after his fourteenth birthday was apprenticed to a sawyer in the Dockyard. Should the attorney not have done better for him? Is there just a touch of Mr Murdstone in the business? But then it seems not. For when Henry grew up and married he called his first (and only) son after his step-father, naming him in full, paying him the warmest tribute he could give. As for his own father, Joseph Carrington about whom I know nothing except that he married Barbary, begat a son, and was dead before she married again, not one of his many male descendants received his name.

Is this significant? It could be—or not. The positive repetition of a name can be real evidence, but a negative fact like this one is only fit for speculation. There is no harm in speculation and it can lead to something fruitful, but it must always be kept separate from facts. The name Nicholas was not continued in my family either, and I know the reason for that. N.T.C., my great-grandfather, was a school-master; he knew the boys spoke of him as Old Nick and he didn't like it. He tried to keep the name dark, never using anything but initials and he didn't give it to any of his seven sons. So it may be that he just didn't like the name of Joseph either. Or it may be that Joseph was better forgotten.

Christian names can provide the lighter side of genealogy and, complete with their surnames, conjure up lively human pictures out of the long-forgotten past. The pictures are probably wrong; to me Rosamund Verant was a charmer and Ann Mudge a good girl but plain; and as likely as not it was the other way round. But the pictures will arise and enliven our researches. Athanasius Jenkyn sounds ponderous if not pompous, but having said so I hasten to send my apologies to my five-times great uncle.

There is pleasure in seeing the fashions of different ages come and go (while the 'steadies', William, John, Ann and Jane never waver): the moral names of the Puritans, not just the few that are still with us such as Prudence and Hope, but sterner stuff like Repentance, Obedience, and worse. These belong mostly to the early seventeenth century and didn't last long, but I have noted the baptism in a Nonconformist register of 1801 of Thankful Smallbones (a boy).

More widely acceptable was the fashion for classical names in the late eighteenth and early nineteenth centuries. For a time Mary gave way to Maria, accompanied by Julia, Sophia and Augusta, while their brothers might be Horace or Septimus. A little later the Victorians preferred to revive the Old English names such as Edith and Hilda, Edwin, Wilfred and the long-neglected Alfred.

It can be amusing to see how some parish clerks whose knowledge of spelling was limited did their best or worst with unfamiliar names, particularly with girls' names which had a variety beyond their ken. Pennellopey is a straightforward rendering of what the clerk heard; Winnifruit made me laugh out loud.

Some people might think that hunting through old lists and indexes is tedious work. So it can be especially if you find nothing to the purpose, but a taste for names can save you. I went once to a village on the Cornish boundary with Devon on the off-chance of finding some of my family. It was a beautiful place where from the vestry window of the church I looked down over wooded slopes to the Tamar. The register was soon searched for the inhabitants had always been few, but I lingered because their names were so delightful. There was a family called Cake, who had intermarried with another called English (which in that region would have meant a foreigner from across the Tamar) and one of the Cake boys was christened English. Another family surnamed Moon gave its daughters charming names like Loveday and Epiphany, and when Epiphany Moon married English Cake my cup of happiness was full. I found no trace of my own forefathers but felt it was a day well spent.

15

General Strategy

Every quest in search of ancestors is different from every other. We set out from different starting points, and the knowledge we carry with us by way of equipment varies infinitely. For some the trail is easy to follow; for others it may vanish without a trace; luck may be with us or against, and the facts that we eventually uncover have all the diversity of human beings.

For this reason it is impossible to advise any particular order of procedure beyond the general rules, already mentioned, of doing what is easiest first, collecting all available material before setting out, working from the known to the unknown, keeping methodical records, and always preparing oneself carefully for each new venture.

One of the chief troubles that the keen amateur genealogist has to contend with—and it is rapidly getting worse—is the cost of travelling and of sometimes having to stay overnight to do a job properly. All hobbies cost something, and most of them much more than genealogy, but you can generally arrange to practise them in your own home town, while there is no controlling your ancestors who may lead you—willy nilly—all over the country. That is unless they were very firmly established in one place for centuries and always married in that neighbourhood. The best people for this point of view were farmers, prosperous enough to make wills, but not too rich because that would make them more mobile. One wants them well tied to their land and their comfortable farmhouse and doing nicely, as very many were in the seventeenth and eighteenth centuries. But the trouble is that we, their descendants, are probably living somewhere quite different.

A great deal can be done in the big record repositories in London, but not everything unless your forbears were all Londoners. Before 1800 the majority of the population lived in the country and sooner or later you will have to

consult the original records to be found only in country churches or provincial record offices. In any case you will want to visit the natural habitat of
your forbears. And unless you are remarkably lucky and efficient you will
probably need to go again. Or maybe nearly everything can be done in one
county, but it would need a first-class reference library as well as its record
office, and you would have to have a good knowledge of three or four
generations to start you off. Few people can do without a visit to the national
record collections in London.

Consequently when you make your plans—and you must keep on planning all the time, constantly adapting your ideas to new developments—you
must do it with a view to saving journeys. This is where preparation comes
in. If you are going some distance to see local records, make sure you
have thought of everything you could do in that district. If you are writing to
a record office to discover the whereabouts of parish registers before you go
(and this is recommended) ask at the same time about local wills and other
special types of record that you want to see.

Many record offices have printed guides to their contents that are quite
inexpensive. If you get one in advance, you may come across some possibility that you hadn't thought of; and if there is something on microfilm
you would like to see, you can ask them to reserve the viewing machine for
you, to avoid disappointment.

The Borthwick Institute in York, for instance, has recently published a
guide book not only to its own fine collection of archives, but also to those
of the other Yorkshire record offices. Anyone hunting for ancestors in the
north of England should bear this in mind.

I have found it useful to keep a notebook of all my special 'wants' as they
occur to me, under the headings of the places where they could be found—
like a shopping list. There are so many small points to be checked and
possibilities to be explored, and some can only be done in one place and some
in another. When I get to a record office or major library I am not likely
to forget my main object but in the excitement of concentrating on that I
could easily forget other essential things that could be done there and
nowhere else. This is what I mean by careful preparation. I said in Chapter 2
that a genealogist's motto might be 'Try Everything'. Another to keep in
mind is 'Be Prepared'.

The difficulty of being often far away from the best source for one's investi-
gations can be partly mitigated by making enquiries by post, and the rising
cost of travel is to some extent counterbalanced by the advance of technology

that has given us photocopying and microfilm. It is a great help that copies of wills can be obtained at a moderate cost from most of the repositories that hold them, whether in London or the provinces. And indexes of wills which are not in print are now available on microfilm in some other places besides the office holding the originals—but not in many places. Chasing wills is still quite an intricate business.

For parish registers nothing takes the place of a personal search. On this matter something has been said on page 36. If it is just a question of establishing one or two facts within a limited date it is quite possible to do it by post, especially if the register is in a record office where the staff are generally very helpful, but with registers one is hardly ever satisfied with one item; it only whets one's appetite to look further and find more.

The answer can be to employ a record searcher, which is not the same as a professional genealogist. You can of course put it all in the hands of a professional if you wish but you will find it very expensive, and though he may be better at getting results than you are, nothing of that sort can be guaranteed. Besides you will miss all the fun and the satisfaction of doing it yourself. But to engage someone already on the spot to go through a particular register or other document for you and to report back according to your directions may be a sensible thing to do if it saves a long journey. Your best course is to write to the appropriate record office and ask if they can recommend someone who will undertake it at a reasonable payment by the hour. In London the Society of Genealogists will recommend a searcher either there or elsewhere. If your problem lies in Scotland the **Scottish Ancestry Research Society** will advise you. For Wales the **National Library of Wales** at Aberystwyth has the largest collection of genealogical records, and an enquiry there will be given helpful attention.

But if possible it is always best to go and see the records for yourself.

Like everything else in this modern age the practical side of genealogical research has changed a great deal recently and is still changing. In Chapter 3 it was explained that many of the records traditionally kept at Somerset House are no longer there. For a time the whole General Register was under threat of being carried off to Lancashire but vigorous action by leading genealogists has prevented this disaster, and saved at least the vital indexes for London.

Then the reorganization of county authorities of 1974 has brought about changes in county record offices. But although some of them now come under new authorities, the actual buildings are still where they were and as yet few of the records they contain have been redistributed. But this changing of ancient boundaries, a matter of which few people know all the details, is an additional reason for checking in advance that the records you want to see are where you would expect them. See pages 123–137.

Fortunately no Act of Parliament can change our ancestors. And if the parish where they lived in Somerset is now officially said to be in Avon, all the contemporary records of their lives will still be headed Somerset and given as Somerset in every index. It is only the question of where you go to see them that needs extra care and forethought.

Although in some ways the search for ancestors has become more complicated and certainly more expensive, yet in other ways it is steadily getting simpler and easier. Every year more parish registers and old documents of every sort are deposited with local authorities and become more readily available to the public. And all the time different classes of records are being catalogued and indexed. The *Genealogists' Magazine* in every quarterly issue has important new works to review, all of them aids to tracing ancestry. If you want to know of the latest books on this subject write to Phillimores (see page 135), the chief genealogical publishers, for their book list.

In recent years interest in family history has increased enormously. There are now many regional societies both here and overseas devoted to this subject, groups of like-minded people among whom ideas and information can be exchanged, talks arranged and books made available. There are also one-name groups tracing particular surnames. Write to the Federation of Family History Societies and to the Guild of One-Name Studies (page 136) for lists and details.

The great and growing enthusiasm for social history of all kinds, especially local history, has resulted in a spate of excellent books about special trades and occupations, special localities, and life at special periods in all classes of society. So as you hunt among the manuscripts for your own forbears, don't concentrate on them too narrowly. A book which is particularly illuminating about setting your family tree in its social and local historical context is *Discover Your Family History* by Don Steel (see book list).

The more you know of your forbears' background, the conditions in which they lived and the problems of their time, the more interest you will find on the faded pages and the more vivid will be the glimpses made of your ancestors. You will constantly be surprised, amused or touched by something you see and the hunt for your ancestors will give you much more than a family tree.

APPENDICES

A

Advice to Visitors from Overseas

If you are planning a trip to Britain, hoping to trace some of your ancestors while you are there, try not to postpone all action till you arrive. Get in touch with elderly relatives before leaving home and write down clearly all the family history they can tell you, as suggested in Chapter 1. Note especially the dates and places of births, marriages and deaths as nearly as possible. In Chapter 3 you can read how much you will need them.

Supposing your great-grandfather migrated overseas in the mid-nineteenth century, you should be able to find his birth in the General Register in London, provided he was born in England or Wales after 1837 and you know the approximate date. If he was born earlier you will need to know the exact place of birth. If he had children born in England after that date, you should be able to find their births (if you know the dates) which will give their parents' address and start you on the trail. So collect all possible facts. It would be very time-wasting to have to write back home for details that you could have noted before you set out.

And there may be other useful information that could be found abroad. In all the English-speaking countries much interest is now taken in their early history, and local societies have sprung up devoted to collecting records of early settlers and pioneers. A few of the principal overseas genealogical societies are listed on pages 141-2 and would advise you of more local ones. But you can probably find them by asking at the principal library or museum of your locality. In some cases passenger lists of early voyages out to colonies have been preserved, and this is more likely in the country of destination than in England, though either is possible.

In London you will be sure to visit the official headquarters of your own country—the American Embassy, Australia House, or whichever it is—each of which has an excellent library of works relating to its own history and catalogues of existing records. In these offices you will also get help in obtaining tickets for such places as the British Museum Library and the Public Record Office.

Don't leave your genealogy all to the end of your trip, thinking that you can polish it off in a couple of weeks. Getting certificates from the General Register (even after you have found the required names) will involve several days' delay, so will enquiries to locate parish registers, and many other procedures, so make a start in good time, even if you leave most of the work till later. Be sure to make advance enquiries to record offices whenever possible as they are sometimes so full in the summer months that you may even be refused admission.

On your visit to Britain you are probably thinking chiefly of your British ancestors, but there may be among them a family who came here from some ither country of whose origin you would like to know more. If so, you may find them among the naturalisation records which, as mentioned on page 27, are now at the Public Record Office at Kew. For the P.R.O. you will need a Reader's Ticket, which must be applied for in advance, so if possible write first, or telephone, setting out your problem, and they will tell you if it is worth your going there.

In family history research the range of the problems you might hope to solve is so wide that a book of this size could not possibly touch on all of them, but if you keep asking and trying you may be surprised at the amount you can discover.

B *Book List*

No attempt has been made to include such well-known standard reference books as the many works on the peerage and landed gentry by Debrett, Burke, Kelly and others, which have flowed in a continuous stream since 1803. (*Debrett's Peerage* of that date was the first, but the Burkes, father and son, give more family history.) Nor are details given of the many directories of the leading professions, or the massive *Dictionary of National Biography*. But it should be noted that separate biographical dictionaries exist for Wales (1959) and Ireland (revised 1937), also for Australia, Canada (in progress), New Zealand and the U.S.A.

Also omitted are the many indexes of wills and marriages published by various bodies for particular courts or regions. They are generally placed together on library shelves or may be enquired for.

The following is a short selection of the books which may be the most useful. For a fuller bibliography, see G. Hamilton-Edwards's *In Search of Ancestry*, which lists many detailed articles from periodicals, as well as more specialized books on genealogical subjects.

Army Lists, printed from 1754. The oldest copies may be found at the P.R.O. at Kew and the B.M. Library (listed under *England* in the B.M. catalogues). (See also under Dalton, Hart.)

Barrow, G. B., *The Genealogist's Guide: an index to printed British pedigrees and family histories, 1950–75*, 1977 (See also Marshall, Whitmore.)

Black, George F., *The Surnames of Scotland, Their Origin, Meaning and History*, New York, 1949

Boase, Frederick, *Modern English Biography*, 1892–1965, reprinted 1965. (Includes many names not in the *Dictionary of National Biography*.)

Boutell, Charles, *English Heraldry*, revised edition 1965

Burke's Dormant and Extinct Peerages, reprinted 1978 (from 1883 edition)

Burke, Sir John B., *The General Armoury of England, Scotland, Ireland and Wales*, reprinted 1962 (Includes extinct arms as well as current ones.)

Camp, Anthony J., *Wills and Their Whereabouts*, 4th edition, 1974

Clare, Wallace, *A Simple Guide to Irish Genealogy*, 3rd edition, 1966

Cox, Jane, and Padfield, Timothy, *Tracing your Ancestors in the Public Record Office*, (H.M.S.O.) 1981

Crawford, D. J., *Roll of the Indian Medical Service, 1615–1930*, 1930

Dalton, Charles, *English Army Lists and Commission Registers, 1661–1714*, 6 volumes, 1892–1904

—— *George I's Army, 1714–1727*, 2 volumes, 1910

Dodwell, Edward, and Miles, J. S., *The East India Company's Civil Servants*, 3 volumes, Bombay, Bengal and Madras, 1839

—— *Officers of the Indian Army, 1764–1837*, 1839

Emmison, Frederick G., *How to Read Local Archives, 1550–1700*, 3rd edition 1971 (A helpful introduction to handwriting of this period.)

—— *Introduction to Archives*, 1977

Fortescue, Sir John, *A History of the British Army*, 13 volumes, 1899–1930. (Well-indexed for names.)

Foster, Joseph, *Index Ecclesiasticus, 1800–1844*, 1890. (An index of clergy.)

—— *Alumni Oxonienses, 1500–1886*, 6 volumes, 1891. (Registers of matriculation at Oxford University.)

—— *The Register of Admissions to Grays Inn, 1521–1889*

Fox Davies, Arthur C., *Armorial Families*, 7th edition 1970

Gibson, J. S. W., *Wills and Where to Find Them*, 1974

Gooder, Eileen, *Latin for Local History, An Introduction*, 1961, 2nd edition 1978

Guppy, H. B., *Homes of Family Names in Great Britain*, 1890, reissued Baltimore, U.S.A., 1968

Hamilton-Edwards, Gerald, *In Search of Ancestry*, 3rd edition 1974

—— *In Search of Army Ancestry*, 1978 (A practical guide to the field of army records from 1600 to the present day.)

—— *In Search of Scottish Ancestry*, 1972

Hart, H. G., *Army List*, 1840–1916

Humphery-Smith, Cecil R., *The Phillimore Atlas and Index of Parish Registers*, 1982

MacLysaght, Edward, *Irish Families, Their Names, Arms and Origins*, 1957 (reissued 1972)

—— *More Irish Families*, 1960

—— *Supplement to Irish Families*, 1964

—— *The Surnames of Ireland*, 1978

McKinley, R. A., *English Surnames Series* (in progress):

Volume 1, *Yorkshire, the West Riding*, 1973
Volume 2, *Norfolk and Suffolk*, 1975
Volume 3, *Oxfordshire*, 1978

Marshall, George, *The Genealogist's Guide*, 4th ed. 1903, reissued 1967. (Goes up to 1903. See also Barrow, Whitmore.)

Martin, C. T., *The Record Interpreter*, 1910

Munro, Robert W., *Kinsmen and Clansmen*, 1971. (Gives the tartans and histories of Scottish clans.)

National Index of Parish Registers, 1971 – in progress (1982)

Volume 1, *Sources of Births, Marriages and Deaths before 1837*
Volume 2, *Sources for Nonconformist Genealogy*
Volume 3, *Sources for Roman Catholic and Jewish Genealogy*
Volume 4, *Kent, Surrey and Sussex*
Volume 5, *South Midlands and Welsh Border*
Volume 11 (Part 1), *Northumberland and Durham*
Volume 12, *Sources for Scottish Genealogy*
(Other volumes in progress)

Navy Lists, first published as *Steel's Navy List* in 1772, and continued more officially from 1814 (listed under *England* in the B.M. catalogue)

O'Byrne, William R., *A Naval Biographical Dictionary, comprising the life and service of every officer in the Royal Navy in 1845*, published 1849

Original Parish Registers in Record Offices and Libraries, 1974, with later supplements (issued by Local Population Studies, of Matlock, Derbyshire)

Papworth, J. W., and Morant, A., *Papworth's Ordinary of British Armorials*, reprinted 1977 (Invaluable for identifying unknown coats of arms.)

Parish Register Copies:
Part 1, *The Society of Genealogists' Collection*, 1975, reissued 1978
Part 2, *Other than the Society's Collection*, 1974, reissued 1978
(Two leaflets, published by the Society of Genealogists.)

Reaney, Percy H., *A Dictionary of British Surnames*, 1958, 2nd edition 1976

Richardson, John, *The Local Historian's Encyclopedia*, 1974. (Full of useful facts about records and how to find them.)

Shaw, William A., *The Knights of England, a complete record from the earliest times*, 2 volumes, 1906

Steel, Don, *Discovering Your Family History* (B.B.C. publication), 1980

Stuart, Margaret, *Scottish Family History*, 1930

Sturgess, H. A. C., *Register of Admissions to the Middle Temple, 1500–1944*, 1949

Unwin, George, *The Guilds and Companies of London*, 2nd edition, 1962

Venn, John, and Venn, J. A., *Alumni Cantabrigienses*, 10 volumes, 1922–1954. (Matriculations to Cambridge University from its earliest times to 1900.)

Wagner, Sir Anthony, *English Genealogy*, 2nd edition, 1972

Walford's County Families of the United Kingdom, 1860–1920

Whitmore, John B., *A Genealogical Guide; an index to British pedigrees in continuation of Marshall's Genealogist's Guide*, 1953. (Covers 1900–1950. See also Barrow, Marshall.)

Who Was Who, 5 volumes, 1897–1959

Willis, Arthur J., *Genealogy for Beginners*, revised edition 1979

★ ★ ★

The Institute of Heraldic and Genealogical Studies, at Northgate, Canterbury, Kent, publishes a series of county maps showing parish boundaries, parish churches and starting dates of their registers, and probate jurisdictions. Also available in volume form.
See also *The Phillimore Atlas and Index of Parish Registers*, under Humphery-Smith, above.

C   *The Will of Henry Hile 1703*

In the Name of God Amen The Sixteenth day of August in the Yeare of our Lord 1703 I Henry Hile of Bridport in the County of Dorsett Yeoman being weake of Body but of Sound and perfect mind and memory praised be God therefore do make & ordaine this my last Will and Testament in manner and forme following First I bequeath my Soul into the hands of Almighty God my Maker hopeing through Jesus Christ my only Saviour to receive free pardon and forgivenesse of all my Sins, and my body to be buried in Christian buriall at the discretion of my Executrix hereafter named Item I give and bequeath unto my Son John Hile Eight pounds Sterling and a brass Crock which was formerly his Grandfathers Item I give unto Joane wife of my Said Son John Hile one Copper pan Item I give unto my daughter Elizabeth Akerman Ten pounds Sterling and one Small Brass pan Item I give unto my daughter Joane Hile Twenty pounds Sterling the Chest in the Chamber of my now dwelling house a Feather Bed whereon She doth usually Ly the Bedstead whereon I do now Ly the Warming pan which was her uncles and Gelly Crocke Five pewter platters of the middle Size and Three Candlesticks one of them Brass and Two of them pewter All which Legacys before mentioned I do Will Shall be paid and delivered within One Yeare next after my decease Item all the rest of my goods and Chattells not before given and bequeathed I do give and bequeath unto my daughter Sarah Hile whom I do hereby appoint to be the whole and Sole Executrix of this my last Will and Testament Item I do Revoke all former Wills by me made In Witnes whereof I have hereunto Sett my hand and Seale the day and Yeare First above written

Signed Sealed published
and declared by the Testator Henry
Hile as and for his last Will and
Testament In the presence of

     Thomas Taylor

     Lionel Browne

The Marke of the Testator

Henry   H   Hile

18 Jan^{ry} 1703 juxta etc
Jurat' fuit executrix
Cor' me
Onesiph. Tompson

See Plate 5 for a photograph of the original Will, now in the Dorset CRO.

D

Address List

The information given was correct at the time this edition was prepared (Autumn 1981) but cannot be guaranteed to remain so. Unless otherwise stated, entrance and search are free.

ENGLAND: Principal Libraries, Record Offices and Repositories

1. IN LONDON

THE BRITISH LIBRARY, The British Museum, Great Russell Street, London WC1B 3DG: 01–636 1544
Reading Room: *Mon, 9.00–5.00; Tues, Wed, Thurs, 9.00–9.00; Fri–Sat, 9.00–5.00*
Map Room: *Mon–Sat, 9.30–4.30*
Reader's ticket essential; application forms available by post or on personal call

BRITISH LIBRARY NEWSPAPER LIBRARY, Colindale Ave, London NW9 5HE: 01–205 6039/ 4788
Mon–Sat, 10.00–5.00
Apply initially to the British Library (entry above), in writing; a long-period British Library ticket also covers entry to the Newspaper Library
Holds the National Collection of newspapers, excepting London papers pre-1801 which are kept at the British Library

GENEALOGISTS, SOCIETY OF, 37 Harrington Gardens, London SW7: 01–373 7054
Mon, closed; Tues, 10.00–6.00; Wed–Thurs, 10.00–8.00; Fri, 10.00–6.00; Sat, 10.00–6.00
Non-members may use library at set fees for half day, whole day, day and eve.
Quarterly journal, free to members; by subscription to non-members

GENERAL REGISTER OFFICE, St Catherine's House, 10 Kingsway, London WC2: 01–242 0262
Mon–Fri, 8.30–4.30
Admittance and search of indexes, free; fees charged for certificates; postal enquiries accepted, given sufficient detail, for fee

GREATER LONDON RECORD OFFICE (London and Middlesex), 40 Northampton Road, London EC1: 01–633 6851
Tues, 10.00–7.30; Wed–Fri, 10.00–4.45

GUILDHALL LIBRARY, Guildhall, London (public entrance, Aldermanbury), EC2P 2EJ: 01–606 3030
Mon–Sat, 9.30–5.00

Newspaper room (files of Times and City Press), Mon–Fri, 9.30–5.00
Brief guide to library holdings available

PRINCIPAL PROBATE REGISTRY, Somerset House, Strand, London WC2: 01–405 7641
Mon–Fri, 10.00–4.30
Admittance and search of indexes, free; small reading charge per Will; photocopies; searches in
  response to postal enquiries, given sufficient detail, for fee

PUBLIC RECORD OFFICE: three repositories –

  1. Chancery Lane, London WC2A 1LR: 01–405 0741
      Mon–Fri, 9.30–5.00; closes Bank hols, and for 2 weeks' stock-taking in October
      Reader's ticket essential; application forms on request; limited search of probate
      records in response to postal enquiries (fees charged)

  2. Kew Repository, Ruskin Ave, Kew, Surrey: 01–876 3444
      Hours and closure as above
      Reader's ticket essential; application forms on request

  3. Land Registry Building, Portugal St, London WC2A 1LR: 01–405 3488
      Hours and closure as above
      Day admission (no reader's ticket required); limited search of census returns in
      response to postal enquiries (fees charged)

2. BEYOND LONDON

PARISH CHURCHES

Addresses will be found in Crockford's Clerical Directory under the town or village
concerned. Fees may be charged for register-searching, depending on the time
taken.

DISTRICT REGISTER OFFICES

See local telephone directory under *Registration of Births, Marriages and Deaths.* Fees
charged for admittance to search indexes. Fees charged for certificates supplied in
response to postal enquiries.

COUNTY RECORD OFFICES

The reorganization of counties which came into effect in April 1974 introduced many
new and unfamiliar names into England and Wales, and the addresses of a number of
record offices changed in consequence, although the actual premises and their
contents remained on the whole as they were. In the cases of cities that became the
administrative centres of new counties there was some movement of documents
needed for local government, but the older records, those most useful for
genealogy, in general remained where they were, though perhaps under a new
authority.
These changes make it doubly advisable to check in advance before going far to visit
any record office that it does have the class of record that you want to see. This
applies particularly to the counties that have suffered much change such as Yorkshire
and Durham. Apart from your own convenience, the office staff (particularly of the
smaller record offices) generally appreciate some notice of your visit. Accom-

modation for spreading out documents may be limited, and as so many records are now available on microfilm the booking of microfilm readers has become an important matter. An advance approach, stating the object of your search as nearly as possible, should prevent delay and disappointment. Write to the Archivist in Charge or telephone the office. An S.A.E. is appreciated and helpful in ensuring a quick answer.

Opening hours vary, as may be seen from the following list. Most record offices close for lunch (not indicated in this list, so it is as well to enquire about this too) although some allow readers to remain during the lunch hour to study documents already supplied. All record offices close on Bank Holidays and many add an extra day to the official holiday. Some record offices have now introduced a system whereby orders for documents etc. are collected and fulfilled only at stated times, often with an hour's interval between them; this affects the planning of readers' work, and is a point to note on arrival.

Admission to most county record offices, but not all, is free. Fees may be charged for production of some documents. Photocopies can be obtained at very moderate prices.

Most record offices undertake, for a fee, limited searches in answer to postal enquiries, provided enough detailed information is supplied. If the query is likely to involve too long a search the staff may recommend a professional searcher.

The use of ink is always forbidden; ballpoint pens may be tolerated, but be sure to have a supply of pencils in case they are not.

All the record offices listed below hold many types of original manuscripts relating to the towns and villages of the county and their past inhabitants. They also have information as to the whereabouts of other records not in their keeping, and their staff will advise you on where else to search.

AVON   *A new county formed from parts of Gloucestershire and Somerset around the city of Bristol; nearly all the records of the old counties remain in their respective offices, see below; see* Bristol *(next section) for the city's own archives*

BEDFORDSHIRE   County Record Office, County Hall, Bedford MK42 9AP: Bedford 63222
Mon–Fri, 9.15–5.00

BERKSHIRE   Berkshire Record Office, Shire Hall, Shinfield Park, Reading RG2 9XD: Reading 85444
Mon, 2.00–5.00; Tues–Wed, 9.00–5.00; Thurs, 9.00–9.00; Fri, 9.00–4.30
Wills proved in Archdeaconry Court of Berkshire (formerly held in Bodleian Library, Oxford) are now at this CRO; parish reg list on request for small charge
See also Oxfordshire *(below),* Oxford *(next section)*

BUCKINGHAMSHIRE   Buckinghamshire Record Office, County Hall, Aylesbury HP20 1UA: Aylesbury 5000
Mon–Thurs, 9.00–5.15; Fri, 9.00–4.45
Parish reg list and Notes for Genealogists *available on request*

CAMBRIDGESHIRE   County Record Office, Shire Hall, Cambridge CB3 0AP: Cambridge 358811
Mon, 9.00–5.15; Tues, 9.00–9.00 (by appt only after 5.15); Wed–Thurs, 9.00–5.15; Fri, 9.00–4.15

Serves Cambridgeshire including Isle of Ely; the former county of Huntingdonshire is served by
a branch office at Huntingdon (see below)
Diocesan and local probate records are housed in the University Library, Cambridge; may be
consulted on written application to University Archivist
Booklet and parish reg list available for small charge
See also Huntingdonshire (below)

CHESHIRE   Cheshire Record Office and Chester Diocesan Record Office, The Castle,
Chester CH1 2DN: Chester 602574 (enquiries), 602560 (County Archivist)
Mon, 9.00–5.00 (1st and 3rd Mons each month, 9.00–9.00; documents must be ordered by
4.30); Tues–Fri, 9.00–5.00; 3 days' notice required
Free leaflet on request; guide available for small charge

CLEVELAND   Cleveland County Archives Dept, 81 Borough Road, Middlesborough,
TS1 3AA: Middlesborough 210944
Mon–Thurs, 9.00–5.00; Fri, 9.00–4.30
Parish records for that part of county which is now in diocese of York; microfilm copies of parish
records for that part of county which is in diocese of Durham (originals in Durham CRO)
Leaflets available on request free of charge

CORNWALL   County Record Office and Diocesan Record Office, County Hall, Truro,
TR1 3AY: Truro 3698
Mon, closed: Tues–Thurs, 9.30–5.00; Fri, 9.30–4.30; Sat, 9.00–12.00; appointment essential
Parish reg list available for small charge

CUMBERLAND   *See Cumbria (below)*
CUMBRIA   *Records of the former counties of Cumberland and Westmorland:*

The Record Office, The Castle, Carlisle: Carlisle 23456
Mon–Fri, 9.00–5.00

Cumbria Record Office, County Offices, Kendal, LA9 4RQ: Kendal 21000
Mon–Fri, 9.00–5.00

Cumbria Record Office, 140 Duke Street, Barrow-in-Furness: Barrow 31269
Mon–Fri, 2.00–5.00; mornings by appointment only

DERBYSHIRE   *Two relevant offices:*

Derbyshire Record Office, County Offices, Matlock, DE4 3AG: Matlock 3411
Mon–Fri, 9.30–4.45; appointment desirable
See also Derby (next section)

Local Studies Dept, address and telephone as CRO above
Mon–Fri, 9.00–5.00
Microfilm of census returns; Mormon microfiche; local studies material

DEVON   *Two offices hold Devon county records:*

Devon Record Office (Headquarters), Castle Street, Exeter, EX4 3PQ: Exeter 53509
Mon–Thurs, 9.30–5.00; Fri, 9.30–4.30; also opens 1st and 3rd Sats except before Bank Hols
Diocesan and city records; appointment preferable; parish reg list; fee for admittance

West Devon Record Office, Clare Place, Coxside, Plymouth: Plymouth 264685

Mon–Thurs, 9.30–5.00; Fri, 9.30–4.30; also opens 2nd Sat of each 2nd month except before Bank Hols
Fee for admittance

DORSET   Dorset Record Office, County Hall, Dorchester, Dorset: Dorchester 63131
Mon–Fri, 9.00–5.00
Parish reg list available for small charge

DURHAM   *Two offices hold relevant archives:*

Durham County Record Office, County Hall, Durham, DH1 5UL: Durham 64411
Mon–Tues, 8.45–4.45; Wed, 8.45–8.30 (documents needed after 4.45 must be ordered in advance); Thurs, 8.45–4.45; Fri, 8.45–4.15
At present, sole repository for parish records of diocese, including area north of the Tees now in Cleveland and area south of the Tyne now in Tyne and Wear; see also Tyne and Wear
Parish record list available on request

The Department of Palaeography and Diplomatic, 5 The College, Durham
Wills and admons of Consistory Court of Durham to 1858; marriage bonds from 1594; bishops' transcripts, c. 1760–c. 1830 (incomplete)
See also Tyne and Wear

ELY, ISLE OF   *See Cambridgeshire*

ESSEX   *There are two Essex record offices:*

Essex Record Office, County Hall, Chelmsford CM1 1LX: Chelmsford 67222
Mon, 10.00–8.45; Tues–Thurs, 9.15–5.15; Fri, 9.15–4.15

Southend Branch Record Office, Central Library, Victoria Avenue, Southend-on-Sea SS2 6EX: Southend 612621
Mon–Thurs, 9.15–5.15; Fri, 9.15–4.15

GLOUCESTERSHIRE   Gloucestershire Record Office, Worcester Street, Gloucester GL1 3DW: Gloucester 21444
Mon–Wed, 9.00–5.00; Thurs, 9.00–8.00; Fri, 9.00–5.00
In addition to usual classes of record, holds diocesan and city records
Leaflet available

GREATER MANCHESTER   *See Manchester (next section) and Lancashire (below)*

HAMPSHIRE   Hampshire Record Office and Winchester Diocesan Record Office, 20 Southgate St, Winchester SO23 9EF: Winchester 63153
Mon–Thurs, 9.00–4.45; Fri, 9.00–4.15; 2nd and 4th Sats except preceding Bank hols, 9.00–11.55 (documents must be ordered in advance)
In addition to usual classes of record, holds archives of Winchester City Record Office; parish reg list available
See also Wight (below), Portsmouth and Southampton (next section)

HEREFORD AND WORCESTER   *These counties have been combined into one:*

Hereford Record Office, The Old Barracks, Harold Street, Hereford HR1 2QZ: Hereford 65441

Mon–Fri, 9.15–4.45
Holds Hereford county and diocesan records; see also Hereford *(nèxt section)*

Worcester Record Office, County Buildings, St Mary's Street, Worcester (apply to County Archivist): Worcester 353366
Mon–Fri, 9.15–4.45

St Helen's Branch Record Office, Fish Street, Worcester (apply to Senior Asst Archivist): Worcester 353366
Mon–Fri, 9.15–4.45
Holds diocesan records for Worcester

HERTFORDSHIRE   Hertfordshire Record Office, County Hall (Room 204), Hertford SG13 8DE: Hertford 54242
Mon–Thurs, 9.15–5.15; Fri, 9.15–4.30

HUMBERSIDE   A new county consisting of parts of Yorkshire and Lincolnshire:

County Record Office, County Hall, Beverley, North Humberside HU17 9BA: Hull 867131
Mon, 9.00–4.45; Tues, 9.00–8.00; Wed–Thurs, 9.00–4.45; Fri, 9.00–4.00
Serves the former East Riding of Yorkshire
Parish reg list available free of charge
See also Hull *(next section)*

South Humberside Area Record Office, Town Hall Square, Grimsby, South Humberside DN31 1HX: Grimsby 53481
Mon, 9.30–5.00; Tues, 9.30–9.00 (after 5.00, by appt only); Wed–Fri, 9.30–5.00
Serves Grimsby and Scunthorpe area; the Lincolnshire Archives Office (see below) is still the sole repository for Lincoln diocesan records

HUNTINGDONSHIRE   *Now incorporated into Cambridgeshire*
County Record Office, Grammar School Walk, Huntingdon PE18 6LF: Huntingdon 52181
Mon–Fri, 9.00–5.00; Sat mornings by special appointment: advance notice appreciated
Booklet from Camb. CRO applies (see Cambridgeshire, *above)*

KENT   Kent Archives Office, County Hall, Maidstone, ME14 1XH: Maidstone 671411
Mon, 9.00–7.30; Tues–Thurs, 9.00–4.30; Fri, closed
Parish reg list, Guide, etc, available for small charge
See also Canterbury, Rochester *(next section)*

LANCASHIRE   Lancashire Record Office, Bow Lane, Preston PR1 8ND: Preston 54868
Mon, closed; Tues, 10.00–8.30; Wed–Fri, 10.00–5.00
Handlist of genealogical sources and Guide available for small charge
See also Liverpool, Manchester *(next section)*

LEICESTERSHIRE   Leicestershire Record Office, 57 New Walk, Leicester LE1 7JB: Leicester 554100
Mon–Thurs, 9.15–5.00; Fri, 9.15–4.45; Sat, 9.15–12.15
Records of former county of Rutland are beginning to be deposited here

LINCOLNSHIRE   Archives Office, The Castle, Lincoln LN1 3AB: Lincoln 25158

Mon–Fri, 9.30–4.45; advance notice required
Bishops' transcripts, parish regs, etc, for the diocese of Lincoln, including that part which is now South Humberside; lists available on request for small charge; SAE with all enquiries

MERSEYSIDE   *See* Lancashire *(above), and* Liverpool *(next section)*

MIDDLESEX   *See* Greater London Record Office *(previous section)*

NORFOLK   Record Office, Central Library, Norwich NR2 1NJ: Norwich 611277
Mon–Fri, 9.00–5.00; Sat, 9.00–12.00: 7 days' advance notice for uncatalogued material; advance appt requested; seats bookable, must be claimed by 9.30
Booklet available for small charge

˙NORTHAMPTONSHIRE   Northamptonshire Record Office, Delapre Abbey, Northampton NN4 9AW: Northampton 62129
Mon–Wed, 9.15–4.45; Thurs, 9.15–7.45 (records needed after 5.00 must be ordered in advance); Fri, 9.15–4.45; Sat, 9.00–12.15 (advance notice essential): appt preferred

NORTHUMBERLAND   County Record Office, Melton Park, North Gosforth, Newcastle upon Tyne NE3 5QX: Wideopen 2680
Mon, 9.00–5.00 (2nd in month, 9.00–9.00); Tues–Thurs, 9.00–5.00; Fri, 9.00–4.30; last Sat in month, 9.00–12.00: advance notice helpful
Parish records and copies of post-1858 wills for the county, including that area, formerly in Northumberland, which is now in Tyne and Wear, although some official records are being transferred to Tyne and Wear Record Office; see also Tyne and Wear *(below)*

NOTTINGHAMSHIRE   Nottinghamshire Record Office and Southwell Diocesan Record Office, County House, High Pavement, Nottingham NG1 1HR: Nottingham 54524
Mon, 9.00–4.45; Tues, 9.00–7.15 (order documents by 6.45); Wed–Thurs, 9.00–4.45; Fri, 9.00–4.15; 1st and 3rd Sats, 9.30–12.45 (last orders for documents, 12.00)
Nottingham City Archives have been transferred to this record office

OXFORDSHIRE   Oxfordshire County Record Office, County Hall, New Road, Oxford OX1 1ND: Oxford 815203
Mon–Thurs, 9.00–5.00; Fri, 9.00–4.00
Deposits for that part of Oxfordshire which was formerly in Berkshire now being received (1982); ecclesiastical parish records remain in Berkshire R.O.; check in advance
Diocesan parish records and wills are held at Bodleian Library, Oxford *(see next section); census returns are at* Oxford Central Library *(see next section)*

RUTLAND   *See* Leicestershire

SHROPSHIRE (Salop)   County Record Office, The Shirehall, Abbey Foregate, Shrewsbury SY2 6ND: Shrewsbury 222406
Mon, 9.00–5.00; Tues–Wed, closed; Thurs, 9.00–5.00; Fri, 9.00–4.00

SOMERSET   Somerset Record Office, Obridge Road, Taunton TA2 7PU: Taunton 87600/78805
Mon–Thurs, 9.00–4.50; Fri, 9.00–4.20; Sat, 9.00–12.15 (appointment essential); advance notice preferred

Diocesan records for Bath and Wells; parish reg list for fee; census returns searched for fee; SAE essential with postal enquiries
See also Bath *(next section)*

STAFFORDSHIRE   Staffordshire Record Office, County Buildings, Eastgate Street, Stafford ST16 2LZ: Stafford 3121
Mon–Thurs, 9.00–5.00; Fri, 9.00–4.30
Parish reg list available
See also Lichfield, next section

Jointly staffed with the record office is another important source:
William Salt Library, address as above: Stafford 52276
Tues–Thurs, 9.30–5.00; Fri, 9.30–4.30; Sat, 9.30–1.00

SUFFOLK   *Two record offices hold Suffolk records:*

Suffolk Record Office (East Suffolk Area), Ipswich Branch, County Hall, St Helen's Street, Ipswich IP4 2JS: Ipswich 55801
Mon–Thurs, 9.00–5.00; Fri, 9.00–4.00; Sat, 9.00–5.00 by appt only; advance notice required (accommodation limited); Guide available for small charge

Suffolk Record Office (West Suffolk Area), Bury St Edmunds Branch, Schoolhall Street, Bury St Edmunds IP33 1RX: Bury St Edmunds 63141
Mon–Thurs, 9.00–5.00; Fri, 9.00–4.00; Sat, 9.00–5.00 (by appt only); advance notice helpful; Guide available for small charge

SURREY   *Two record offices hold Surrey records:*

Surrey Record Office, County Hall, Kingston upon Thames KT1 2DN: 01–546 1050
Mon–Wed, 9.30–4.45; Thurs, 1.45–4.45; Fri, 9.30–4.45; 2nd and 4th Sats, by advance appt to be made by 12.30 preceding Thurs, 9.30–12.30
Holds parish records for the diocese of Southwark, and for the deaneries of Emly and Epsom in the diocese of Guildford; civil parish records (eg. vestry books) for the whole county

Guildford Muniment Room, Castle Arch, Guildford GU1 3SX: Guildford 573942
Tues–Fri, 9.30–4.45; 1st and 3rd Sats by advance appointment to be made by 12.30 preceding Thurs, 9.30–12.30; advance notice essential
Holds parish records for parishes in the diocese of Guildford, except deaneries of Emly and Epsom (above)

SUSSEX   *In 1974 Sussex was divided into West Sussex and East Sussex, each with its own record office:*

County Record Office, Pelham House, St Andrews Lane, Lewes, East Sussex BN7 1UN: Lewes 5400
Mon–Thurs, 8.45–4.45; Fri, 8.45–4.15

West Sussex County Record Office and Chichester Diocesan Record Office, County Hall, Chichester, West Sussex PO19 1RN: Chichester 785100
Mon–Fri, 9.15–5.00. 3 days' advance notice preferred

TYNE AND WEAR   *Virtually all the genealogical material relating to the new county of Tyne and Wear is still held in the county record offices of Durham and Northumberland (see above): enquire there first; see also address overleaf, and* Newcastle *(next section)*

Tyne and Wear Archives Department, Blandford House, West Blandford St, Newcastle upon Tyne NE1 4JA: Newcastle 326789
Mon, 8.45–5.15; Tues, 8.45–8.30; Wed-Fri, 8.45–5.15
Official records for the new metropolitan county area; microfilm of parish regs (originals in Northumberland CRO and Durham CRO)

WARWICKSHIRE   County Record Office, Priory Park, Cape Road, Warwick CV34 4JS: Warwick 493431 (Mon–Fri), Warwick 42863 (Sats)
Mon–Thurs, 9.00–5.30; Fri, 9.00–5.00; Sat, 9.00–12.30
See also Birmingham, Coventry *(next section)*

WEST MIDLANDS   *See* Birmingham *(next section)*

WESTMORLAND   *See* Cumbria *(above)*

WIGHT, ISLE OF   County and Diocesan Record Office, 26 Hillside, Newport, Isle of Wight PO30 2EB: Newport 524031
Mon–Tues, 9.30–5.00; Wed, 9.30–8.30; Thurs–Fri, 9.30–5.00

WILTSHIRE   County Record Office, County Hall, Trowbridge, Wiltshire: Trowbridge 3641
Mon–Tues, 9.00–5.00; Wed, 9.00–8.30; Thurs–Fri, 9.00–5.00
Leaflet available on request

WORCESTERSHIRE   *See* Hereford and Worcester *(above)*

YORKSHIRE   *In 1974 Yorkshire was divided into three new counties, North, South and West Yorkshire; see also* Cleveland *and* Humberside *(above)*

North Yorkshire County Record Office, County Hall, Northallerton, North Yorkshire DL7 8AD: Northallerton 3123
Mon–Tues, 9.00–4.50; Wed, 9.00–8.50; Thurs, 9.00–4.50; Fri, 9.00–4.20
Advance appointment essential; charge for admittance

West Yorkshire County Record Office, County Hall, Wakefield, West Yorkshire WF1 2QW: Wakefield 67111
Mon–Thurs, 9.00–5.00; Fri, 9.00–4.00; or by special appointment
Diocesan record office for Wakefield; deeds registry since 1704; Guide available for fee

South Yorkshire Record Office, County Cultural Activities Centre, Ellin Street, Sheffield S1 4PL: Sheffield 29191
Mon–Thurs, 9.00–5.00; Fri, 9.00–4.00; appointment advisable
Microfilm of census returns 1841–81; probate calendars 1858–1928; microfilm of bishops' transcripts; microfiche of CFI for Yorkshire; some nonconformist records

See also Bradford, Hull, Leeds, Sheffield *and in particular* York (Borthwick Institute) *(next section)*

CITY, BOROUGH AND DIOCESAN ARCHIVES

Every large city and historic old town has a collection of its own records of its former citizens and their activities, often including some of its original parish registers, copies of census returns, etc. These are generally kept in its principal library, and a selection of the most notable of these civic libraries is listed below.

Cathedral cities formerly kept all their ecclesiastical records, including bishops' transcripts, local wills, and other useful genealogical material, in their diocesan offices, but nearly all have now handed over their older archives to the appropriate County Record Offices, as indicated in the previous section. A few that remained separate are given here.

BATH   The City Archivist, Guildhall, Bath BA1 5AW: Bath 61111
Mon–Thurs, 8.30–5.00; Fri, 8.30–4.30
Records of city parishes; local Methodist records; City Council Records; archival material relating to city and surrounding area

BIRMINGHAM   Local Studies and Archives Dept, Birmingham Reference Library, Chamberlain Sq., Birmingham B3 3HQ: 021–235 4220 (local studies), 4217 (archives)
Mon, 9.00–6.00; Tues–Thurs, 9.00–8.00; Fri, 9.00–6.00; Sat, 9.00–5.00
Diocesan record office for Birmingham; wills 1858–1941; census returns 1841–81; local archives

BRADFORD   Archives and Local Studies Depts, Bradford Central Library, Princes Way, Bradford BD1 1NN: Bradford 33081
Archives: *Mon–Fri, 9.00–5.00*
Local Studies: *Mon–Fri, 9.00–8.00; Sat, 9.00–5.00*
Metropolitan district archives, parish regs, census returns, newspapers, M.I. records

BRISTOL   The City Archivist, Bristol Record Office, The Council House, College Green, Bristol BS1 5TR: Bristol 26031
Mon–Thurs, 8.45–4.45; Fri, 8.45–4.15; Sat by appt only, 9.00–12.00; advance notice preferred
Records of city and diocese of Bristol

CANTERBURY   The Archivist, Cathedral Archives and Library, The Precincts, Canterbury, Kent CT1 2EG: Canterbury 63510
Mon–Fri, 9.30–4.30; closed one week each Jan, April, July, Oct, and sometimes also on Mons during holiday months: advance notice essential
Hourly or daily fees charged for production of parish regs and bishops' transcripts
Letter of recommendation preferred

CHESTER   *See* Cheshire *(previous section)*

COVENTRY   Local Studies Centre, Room 220, Broadgate House, Broadgate, Coventry
Mon–Thurs, 8.45–4.45; Fri, 8.45–4.15; advance notice preferred

DERBY   Derby Local Studies Library, Central Library, The Wardwick, Derby DE1 1HS: Derby 31111
Mon–Fri, 9.00–7.00; Sat, 9.00–12.00

EXETER   *See* Devon *(preceding section)*

HEREFORD   Hereford Library, Broad St, Hereford HR4 9AU: Hereford 2456/68645
Mon, closed; Tues–Wed, 9.30–6.00; Thurs, 9.30–5.00; Fri, 9.30–8.00; Sat, 9.30–4.00
Holds material useful to study of local and family history

HULL, KINGSTON UPON   The City Archivist, 79 Lowgate, Kingston upon Hull, North Humberside, HU1 2AA: Hull 222015/6
Mon–Fri, 8.30–5.00: advance notice requested

LEEDS   *Two relevant addresses are:*

Archives Dept, Sheepscar, Chapeltown Road, Leeds LS7 3AP: Leeds 628339
Mon–Fri, 9.30–5.00: advance notice necessary (7 days for some papers)
Leaflets available free on request

Leeds Reference Library, Central Library, Leeds 1
Holds all printed and microfilmed genealogical records for the city

LICHFIELD   Lichfield Joint Record Office, Lichfield Library, Bird Street, Lichfield, Staffs WS13 6PN: Lichfield 56787
Mon–Tues, 10.00–5.15; Wed, 10.00–4.45; Thurs–Fri, 10.00–5.15; appointment preferred
Diocesan, probate and Church Commissioners' records; bishops' transcripts

LIVERPOOL   Liverpool Record Office, Liverpool City Libraries, William Brown Street, Liverpool L3 8EW: 051–207 2147
Mon–Fri, 9.00–9.00; Sat, 9.00–5.00

MANCHESTER   *Two relevant addresses are:*

Archives Dept, Manchester Public Libraries, Central Library, St Peter's Square, Manchester M2 5PD: 061–236 9422
Mon, 9.00–9.00; Tues–Fri, 9.00–5.00

Local History Library; address as above
Mon–Fri, 9.00–9.00; Sat, 9.00–5.00
Microfilm and/or printed copies of most diocesan parish regs and many in surrounding area; also non-parochial registers; Manchester census returns, 1841–81

NEWCASTLE UPON TYNE   Newcastle Central Library, Newcastle upon Tyne, NE99 1MC: Newcastle 610691
Northumberland and Durham parish regs to 1812 (incomplete); Boyd's marriage index to 1812 (incomplete); index Durham marriage bonds 1594–1815; microfilm of census returns for Newcastle 1841–81; microfiche of CFI for Northumberland and Durham

NOTTINGHAM   *See* Nottinghamshire *(previous section)*

OXFORD   *Two relevant addresses are:*

Bodleian Library, Oxford OX1 3BG: Oxford 44675
Reader's ticket required; application form on request
Holds diocesan records excluding tithes (C.R.O.) but including ecclesiastical parish records and wills; see also Berkshire *(previous section)*

Central Library, Westgate, Oxford, OX1 1DJ: Oxford 815749/722422
Mon–Wed, 9.15–7.00; Thurs, 9.15–5.00; Fri, 9.15–7.00; Sat, 9.15–5.00
Microfilm of census returns 1841–81 for Oxfordshire and former North Berkshire parishes; microfilm reader must be booked in advance
Library also administers Oxford City archives (at least one day's notice is required for their production)

PORTSMOUTH   City Record Office, 3 Museum Road, Portsmouth PO1 2LE: Portsmouth 829765
Mon–Wed, 9.30–5.00; Thurs, 9.30–7.00; Fri, 9.30–4.00

ROCHESTER   Diocesan Registry, The Precinct, Rochester, Kent: Medway 43231
By appointment only

SHEFFIELD   Dept of Local History and Archives, Central Library, Surrey Street, Sheffield S1 1XZ: Sheffield 734753
Mon–Fri, 9.00–5.30; Sat, 9.00–5.00: advance notice essential on Sats
Reprint of account of collections held available

SOUTHAMPTON   Civic Record Office, Civic Centre, Southampton SO9 4XL: Southampton 23855
Mon–Fri, 9.00–5.00; late evenings by prior arrangement only
Parish regs, street directories, etc.

SUTTON COLDFIELD   Reference Library, Lower Parade, Sutton Coldfield, West Midlands B72 1YA: 021–354 2302
Mon–Fri, 9.00–8.00; Sat, 9.00–5.00

WINCHESTER   *See* Hampshire *(previous section)*

WORCESTER   *See* Hereford and Worcester *(previous section)*

YORK   *Useful addresses are as follows:*

Borthwick Institute, St Anthony's Hall, York YO1 2PW: York 59861
Mon–Fri, 9.30–5.00 (closed 2 weeks each year; check in advance); accommodation limited, advance notice essential; new readers must complete application form on arrival
Ecclesiastical archives of archbishopric of York, including probate records of Prerogative Court of York and of diocesan archdeaconries; many parish regs, transcripts, marriage bonds, etc, for Province; leaflet available free of charge on receipt of SAE

York Archives, Exhibition Square, York YO1 2EW
Mon, closed; Tues–Thurs, 9.30–5.30; Fri, closed; Sat, closed; advance appt essential

3.   OTHER USEFUL ADDRESSES

BAPTIST HISTORICAL SOCIETY AND BAPTIST UNION LIBRARY   4 Southampton Row, London WC1B 4AB: 01–405 9803
Advance appointment essential, written applications only; holds records relating to Baptist ministers, but few other records bearing on family history

CATHOLIC RECORD SOCIETY   The Honorary Secretary, Catholic Record Society, c/o 114 Mount Street, London W1Y 6AH
The Society's printed records and registers may be ordered through the public library system, or purchased direct from Wm Dawson & Sons Ltd, Cannon House, Folkestone, Kent; catalogue available for fee; written enquiries re sources and bibliographical information to Secretary with large SAE: no searches undertaken

CHURCH OF JESUS CHRIST OF LATTER-DAY SAINTS, GENEALOGICAL SOCIETY OF   65 Severn Road, Ipswich, Suffolk IP3 0PU: Ipswich 78686
Family pedigrees and histories, international genealogical indexes, etc. See page 44.

COLLEGE OF ARMS   Queen Victoria Street, London EC4V 4BT: 01–248 2762
Mon–Fri, 10.00–4.00
The College's records are not open to the public; enquirers should write to the Officer in Waiting or call at the College with details; search fees charged, according to time taken and nature of work involved

DOCTOR WILLIAMS'S LIBRARY   14 Gordon Square, London WC1H 0AG: 01–387 3727
For Nonconformist records, more particularly Presbyterian/Unitarian, Congregational; advance appointment essential

FAMILY HISTORY SOCIETIES   *See page 136*

HUGUENOT SOCIETY   *For details of membership and use of library, write to the Secretary, c/o Barclays Bank, Pall Mall, London SW1*

IMPERIAL WAR MUSEUM   Lambeth Road, London SE1 6HZ: 01–735 8922
Reference Departments, Mon–Fri, 10.00–5.00; appointment essential
No official personnel records but extensive collection of unit histories, diaries, memoirs, reference works; excellent for background information on World Wars I and II, and military operations since 1914

INDIA OFFICE LIBRARY AND RECORDS   197 Blackfriars Road, London SE1 8NG: 01–928 9531
Mon–Fri, 9.30–6.00; Sat, 9.30–1.00
Admission by ticket; application forms on request

INSTITUTE OF HERALDIC AND GENEALOGICAL STUDIES   Northgate, Canterbury, Kent CT1 1BA: Canterbury 68664/62618
Mon–Fri, 9.00–6.00; Sat by appointment
Academic institute providing facilities for training and post-graduate research in structure and history of the family; arranges non-certificate and diploma courses for amateurs throughout the country; also residential weekend, day, and home study correspondence courses; details from Registrar
Comprehensive genealogical and heraldic libraries; special collections, particularly for London, Kent, Sussex and Hampshire; indexes to parochial and other records for the British Isles in which searches can be undertaken
Publishes journal, series of parish maps, and other aids

JEWISH MUSEUM   Woburn House, Upper Woburn Place, London WC1H 0EP: 01–387 3081/2
Mon–Thurs, 12.30–3.00; Sun, 10.30–12.45

KELLY'S DIRECTORIES LTD   Windsor Court, East Grinstead House, East Grinstead, West Sussex RH19 1XB
Reference library and archives held by IPC Business Press Ltd, Quadrant House, The Quadrant, Sutton, Surrey; 01–661 3500; records not open to public; searches undertaken for a fee, depending on nature of enquiry and time taken

MANORIAL DOCUMENTS REGISTER   The Royal Commission on Historical MSS, Quality
  House, Quality Court, Chancery Lane, London WC2A 1HP
  Mon–Fri, 9.30–5.00; enquire by letter or in person

MANORIAL SOCIETY OF GREAT BRITAIN   65 Belmont Hill, London SE13 5AX: 01–852 0200
  *Comprehensive index of manors, lords and stewards; searches made; some historical material
  provided*

METHODIST ARCHIVES AND RESEARCH CENTRE   Correspondence to the Methodist Con-
  nexional Archivist, c/o the Property Division, Central Hall, Oldham Street,
  Manchester M1 1JQ
  *The Centre can supply lists of stations and copies of the official archives of ministers who died in
  service; other Methodist family research is restricted to supplying obituary notices from the
  denominational magazines (indexed); Methodist baptismal and marriage regs are now
  housed in PRO (London) or county record offices*
  The Methodist Library is housed at John Rylands University Library, Deansgate, Manchester

MORMONS   *See* Church of Jesus Christ of Latter Day Saints *(above)*

NATIONAL ARMY MUSEUM   Department of Records, Reading Room, Royal Hospital
  Road, London SW3 4HT: 01–730 0717
  Tues–Sat, 10.00–4.30
  Admission by reader's ticket, available on written application to Director
  *British and Indian Army lists of commissioned officers; biographical index of officers of the East
  India Company and Indian Armies; casualty lists for Crimean and Boer Wars; location lists
  of British regiments; minimal material on Other Ranks*

NATIONAL MARITIME MUSEUM   London SE10 9NF: 01–858 4422
  Reading room: Mon–Fri, 10.00–5.00; Sat, by appointment only; closes 3rd week in Feb
  *General shipping history; company histories; Lloyd's Registers, Lloyd's Lists, Weekly
  Shipping Indexes, Lloyd's Registers of Shipping (19th century), Wreck Register of Board of
  Trade (1855–1898); plans of merchant vessels, prints and photographs, staff records of some
  shipping companies; some records of Reg-Gen. of Shipping and Seamen (masters' certs,
  indentures, crew lists, etc.)*

NAVY RECORDS SOCIETY   c/o Royal Naval College, Greenwich, London SE10
  *No library or archives; cannot undertake research for enquirers; publishes editions of documents
  relating to British Naval history, which are issued free to members*

PHILLIMORE & CO LTD   Shopwyke Hall, Chichester, Sussex: Chichester 787636
  Principal genealogical publishers; catalogues on request – write, naming your areas of interest

SOCIETY OF FRIENDS   Friends House, Euston Road, London NW1 2BJ: 01–387 3601
  Mon–Fri, 10.00–5.00: closed 1 week spring and August; advance appointment preferred
  *Library open to researchers; small hourly charge; searches undertaken for enquirers at hourly
  charges, but there is normally several months' delay*

UNITARIAN HISTORICAL SOCIETY   6 Ventnor Terrace, Edinburgh EH9 2BL
  *No specific genealogical records; general historical background only; annual magazine available
  to members; the Society's library forms part of the general collection at Dr Williams's
  Library, London (see above)*

UNITED REFORMED CHURCH HISTORY SOCIETY   86 Tavistock Place, London WC1H 9RT:
    01–837 7661
  *Library open by appointment only 10.30–4.00 some weekdays; advance notice essential; limited
  number Presbyterian baptismal regs; some archival material re ministers and missionaries;
  some printed information re Congregational ministers; postal enquiries accepted, small charge
  made*

4.   FAMILY HISTORY SOCIETIES

  In recent years, a considerable number of family history societies have been founded in
  Britain and overseas. These societies guide and encourage members in tracing and
  recording their family histories. Some are regionally based (eg. Cornwall F.H.S.,
  Folkestone F.H.S.), others are 'one-name' (eg. Swinnerton, Talbot). Their finances
  are usually limited to subscriptions, plus perhaps the sale of publications. Some will
  undertake modest searches of local records in return for donations, but others, with
  limited resources at their disposal, can help members only. When writing with any
  enquiry, always send return postage or International Reply Coupons, and a self-
  addressed label. The Federation of Family History Societies, founded in 1974, links
  the member societies and fosters co-operation between national, regional and one-
  name groups throughout the world. Its address is given below. Write for full list.

FEDERATION OF FAMILY HISTORY SOCIETIES   96 Beaumont St, Milehouse, Plymouth
    PL2 3AQ

GUILD OF ONE-NAME STUDIES   15 Cavendish Gdns, Cranbrook, Ilford, Essex IG1 3EA

WALES: Principal Addresses

In 1974 the thirteen former Welsh counties were regrouped into six new ones, or eight if
    you count the three parts of Glamorgan separately. Their 'new' names were those
    of their respective regions in very ancient times.
Bear in mind that the civil registration of Welsh births, marriages and deaths since 1837
    is included with those of England in the General Register in London. All Welsh wills
    since 1858, and those that were proved in the P.C.C. before that date, are also in
    London.

THE NATIONAL LIBRARY OF WALES   The Librarian, National Library of Wales,
    Aberystwyth, Dyfed SY23 3BU: Aberystwyth 3816/7
  Mon–Fri, 9.30–6.00; Sat, 9.30–5.00
  Reader's ticket required; apply in writing several days in advance
  *Diocesan records from all Welsh dioceses, including bishops' transcripts; parish regs of over
  400 parishes; wills proved at Welsh ecclesiastical courts pre-1858*
  *The National Library also acts as a record office for Powys (the former counties of Brecknock-
  shire, Radnorshire, and Montgomeryshire)*

ANGLESEY   *See* Gwynedd *(below)*

BRECKNOCKSHIRE   *See* National Library of Wales *(above)*

CAERNARVONSHIRE *See* Gwynedd *(below)*

CARDIGANSHIRE *See* Dyfed *(below)*

CARMARTHENSHIRE *See* Dyfed *(below)*

CLWYD *Two Clwyd offices hold records from the former counties of Flintshire and Denbighshire:*

County Record Office, The Old Rectory, Hawarden, Deeside, Clwyd CH5 3NR: Hawarden 532364
Mon–Thurs, 9.00–4.45; Fri, 9.00–4.15
Records for former county of Flintshire; some records for Denbighshire

County Record Office, 46 Clwyd Street, Ruthin, Clwyd LL15 1HP: Ruthin 3077
Mon–Thurs, 9.00–4.45; Fri, 9.00–4.15
Records of former county of Denbighshire

DENBIGHSHIRE *See* Clwyd *(above)*

DYFED *Three Dyfed offices hold records of former counties of Cardigan, Carmarthen and Pembroke:*

Cardiganshire Record Office, Swyddfa'r Sir, Marine Terrace, Aberystwyth, Dyfed: Aberystwyth 617581
Mon–Thurs, 9.00–4.45; Fri, 9.00–4.15: advance notice to Carmarthen (next entry)
Records for former county of Cardigan

Carmarthenshire Record Office, County Hall, Carmarthen, Dyfed, SA31 1JP: Carmarthen 31867
Mon–Thurs, 9.00–4.45; Fri, 9.00–4.15; 1st and 3rd Sats (except Bank Holiday weekends), 9.30–12.30 by appointment only
Records for former county of Carmarthenshire; holds most Carmarthenshire parish regs

Pembrokeshire Record Office, The Castle, Haverfordwest, Dyfed SA61 2EF: Haverfordwest 3707
Mon–Thurs, 9.00–4.45; Fri, 9.00–4.15; 1st and 3rd Sats (except Bank Holiday weekends) 9.30–12.30
Records for former county of Pembroke; about 90 Pembrokeshire parish regs

FLINTSHIRE *See* Clwyd *(above)*

GLAMORGAN Glamorgan Record Office, County Hall, Cathays Park, Cardiff CF1 3NE: Cardiff 28033
Tues–Thurs, 9.00–5.00; Fri, 9.00–4.30: advance notice necessary for some collections
In addition to parish records, administers archive collection of former City Lib., Cardiff (now County of S. Glamorgan Lib.)

Pending establishment of an area office in Swansea, temporary facilities provided (1981) third Thurs of each month; advance notice essential; enquire at Cardiff in advance

GWENT County Record Office, County Hall, Cwmbran NP4 2XH: Cwmbran 67711
Mon–Thurs, 9.30–5.00; Fri, 9.30–4.00
Holds records for former county of Monmouthshire, parish regs, etc.

GWYNEDD   *Useful addresses are as follows:*

Caernarfon Area Record Office, Gwynedd Archives Service, County Offices, Shire-hall Street, Caernarfon LL55 1SH: Caernarfon 4121
Mon–Tues, 9.30–5.00; Wed, 9.30–7.00; Thurs, 9.30–5.00; Fri, 9.30–4.00
Central administration of Gwynedd Archives service; documents for the area housed in the offices listed below include parish regs, census returns, voters' lists, rate books, etc.

Gwynedd Archives Service, Area Record Office, Shire Hall, Llangefni, Gwynedd LL77 7TW: Llangefni 723262
Mon–Fri, 9.00–5.00

Area Record Office for Anglesey; enquire at Caernarfon, above

Area Record Office, Penarlag, Dolgellau: Dolgellau 422341
Mon–Fri, 9.30–5.00

Area Record Office for former county of Merioneth; enquire at Caernarfon, above

MERIONETHSHIRE   *See* Gwynedd *(above)*

MONMOUTHSHIRE   *See* Gwent *(above)*

MONTGOMERYSHIRE   *See* National Library of Wales *(above)*

PEMBROKESHIRE   *See* Dyfed *(above)*

POWYS   *See* National Library of Wales *(above)*

RADNORSHIRE   *See* National Library of Wales *(above)*

SOUTH WALES FAMILY HISTORY SOCIETY   18 Clos Ton Mawr, Rhiwbina, Cardiff CF4 6RH
Members meet once a month in Cardiff.

SCOTLAND: Principal Addresses

There are no county record offices in Scotland. Its records are largely concentrated in Edinburgh where its two most important repositories are close together in Princes Street.

THE SCOTTISH RECORD OFFICE   PO Box 36, H.M. General Register House, Edinburgh EH1 3YY: 031–556 6585
Mon–Fri, 9.00–4.45
Admission by ticket on completion of application form; limited searches undertaken for fee
Legal registers including the principal collection of Scottish wills; Church of Scotland records, photocopies of Catholic parish regs prior to 1855, etc.

GENERAL REGISTER OFFICE FOR SCOTLAND   New Register House, Edinburgh EH1 3YT: 031–556 3952
Mon–Thurs, 9.30–4.30; Fri, 9.30–4.00
Admission by ticket, on completion of application form; accommodation limited, admission may be restricted

Departments in this office include: general register of births, marriages and deaths from 1855; Scottish parish regs (1553–1854), series far from complete but contains over 4000 vols; census returns for 1841–91; service records from 1881

Fees charged to search indexes; fees charged to supply certificates or extracts from registers in answer to postal enquiries

For further details, write for leaflet and sheet of charges

COURT OF THE LORD LYON   address as above: 031–556 7255
Mon–Fri, 10.00–4.00
No ticket required; fees charged for searches by members of public
Public Register of all Arms and Bearings in Scotland; public register of Genealogies and Birthbrieves in Scotland

THE NATIONAL LIBRARY OF SCOTLAND   George IV Bridge, Edinburgh EH1 1EW: 031–226 4531
Mon–Fri, 9.30–8.30; Sat, 9.30–1.00
Admission to the reading room by ticket, on completion of application form
Unrivalled collection of Scottish printed works and manuscripts

THE SCOTS ANCESTRY RESEARCH SOCIETY   3 Albany St., Edinburgh EH1 3PY: 031–556 4220
Research into Scottish ancestry and family history

THE SCOTTISH GENEALOGY SOCIETY   The Membership Secretary, 17 Lockharton Gdns, Edinburgh EH14 1AU
Exists to promote research into Scottish family history; publishes quarterly magazine, The Scottish Genealogist, also pre-1855 M.I. lists; library service for U.K. members; register of members' interests; no searches undertaken

NORTHERN IRELAND

GENERAL REGISTER OFFICE   Oxford House, 49–55 Chichester Street, Belfast BT1 4HL: Belfast 35211
Mon–Fri, 9.30–3.30; closed Bank Holidays, including March 17 and July 12–13
Register for births and deaths since 1864; marriages since 1922; for information on R.C. marriages 1864–1922, and other marriages 1845–1922, write to District Registrar, c/o G.R.O., address as above
Indexes open to public; search fees charged; copies of certificates supplied for fee; searches carried out for postal enquiries, given sufficient detail, for fee; leaflet and list of charges available on request

PUBLIC RECORD OFFICE OF NORTHERN IRELAND   66 Balmoral Avenue, Belfast BT9 6NY: Belfast 661621
Mon–Fri, 9.30–4.30; closed on Bank holidays (see above)
Appointment necessary; no searches undertaken (excepting the simplest and briefest looking-up)
For genealogical searches, write to the Secretary of the Ulster Historical Foundation, c/o the P.R.O.; registration fee charged; thereafter fees according to time spent

EIRE

OIFIG AN ARD-CHLARAITHEORA   Custom House, Dublin 1: Dublin 742961
Mon–Fri, 9.30–5.00; closed on public holidays
*Indexes open to public for fee; postal enquiries accepted for fee, given sufficient detail; list of fees
and of records held (almost all being post-1863) available on request*

THE GENEALOGICAL OFFICE   Dublin Castle, Dublin 2

THE PROBATE OFFICE   Four Courts, Dublin 7

THE PUBLIC RECORD OFFICE   Four Courts, Dublin 7

THE NATIONAL LIBRARY   Kildare Street, Dublin 2; *admission by ticket only*

*Baptismal records and other Church records made by the clergy before civil registration began in the
mid-19th century must be pursued via the parish clergy, although the National Library (see
above) holds microfilm of some registers*

THE IRISH GENEALOGICAL RESEARCH SOCIETY   The Secretary, Glenholm High Oakham
Road, Mansfield, Notts, U.K.
Membership fee; annual journal; unpublished source material

THE CHANNEL ISLANDS AND THE ISLE OF MAN

JERSEY

STATES OFFICE   Royal Square, Jersey (The Registrar General)
*Records at the States Office are not open to the public, but postal enquiries may be dealt with,
given sufficient detail*

SOCIETE JERSIAISE   Lord Coutanche Library, 7 Pier Road, St Helier, Jersey: 0534 30538
A private society whose records may be examined by appointment with the librarian

GUERNSEY, ALDERNEY, SARK

THE GREFFE   The Royal Court House, Guernsey: 0481 25277
Mon–Fri, 9.00–4.00
*Admittance by application to Her Majesty's Greffier, at above address; written enquiries dealt
with as resources permit*
*Registers of births, marriages and deaths from 1840 to the present (including Alderney and Sark
from 1924); judicial administrative and land registry records from the mid-16th century, the
majority being in French, open to bona fide-researchers by appointment*

CHANNEL ISLANDS F.H.S.   c/o La Société Jérsiaise, 9 Pier Road, St Helier, Jersey

ISLE OF MAN

GENERAL REGISTRY   Finch Road, Douglas, Isle of Man: Douglas 3358
Mon–Fri, 9.00–4.30
Parish registers pre-1878, and indexes of births, marriages and deaths after 1877, available free of charge; certificates supplied for fee; searches in statutory records may be undertaken for fee, given sufficient information; initial enquiries re wills and deeds; list of records held and fees charged available for SAE

MANX MUSEUM   Crellin's Hill, Douglas, Isle of Man
Microfilm of Manx parish regs, wills, marriage settlements, land deeds, etc; newspapers, books, maps

ISLE OF MAN F.H.S.   The Old Manse, Kirk Michael, Isle of Man

OVERSEAS

A number of the organizations listed below only accept enquiries from their members. Their addresses are included here in case readers, or their relatives overseas, wish to enquire about membership.

AUSTRALIA

AUSTRALIAN INSTITUTE OF GENEALOGICAL STUDIES   PO Box 68, Oakleigh, Victoria 3166
Research is undertaken for members only, and answers to postal enquiries are restricted to suggesting possible sources; the library holds Australiana, with a nucleus of overseas genealogical records (principally relating to the U.K.)

SOCIETY OF AUSTRALIAN GENEALOGISTS   Richmond Villa, 120 Kent Street, Observatory Hill, Sydney, N.S.W. 2000
Reference library open for research to members only, Tues–Thurs, 11.00–4.00; Sat, 11.00–4.00; non-members admitted on payment of search fee per day; quarterly journal
Card index of early settlers; microfilm and microfiche collection; family history repository

CANADA

PUBLIC ARCHIVES OF CANADA   395 Wellington, Ottawa K1A 0N3
Limited searches of indexes undertaken in response to postal enquiries with sufficient detail; booklet listing possible sources (Tracing your Ancestors in Canada) available free

Provincial Societies are as follows:

ALBERTA GENEALOGICAL SOCIETY   Box 12015, Edmonton, Alberta T5J 3L2
BRITISH COLUMBIA GENEALOGICAL SOCIETY   Box 94371, Richmond, B.C. V6Y 2A8
MANITOBA GENEALOGICAL SOCIETY   Box 2066, Winnipeg, Manitoba R3C 3R4
NEW BRUNSWICK GENEALOGICAL SOCIETY   PO Box 3235, Station B, Fredericton, N.B. E3A 2W0

NOVA SCOTIA HISTORICAL SOCIETY   Genealogical Committee, 57 Primrose Street,
    Dartmouth N.S. B3A 4C6
ONTARIO GENEALOGICAL SOCIETY   Box 66, Station Q, Toronto, Ontario, M4T 2L7
PRINCE EDWARD ISLAND GENEALOGICAL SOCIETY   Box 2744, Charlottetown, P.E.I.
    C1A 8C4
QUEBEC FAMILY HISTORY SOCIETY   PO Box 1026, Pointe Claire, Quebec, H9S 4H9
SASKATCHEWAN GENEALOGICAL SOCIETY   Box 1894, Regina, Sask., S4P 3E1

NEW ZEALAND

NEW ZEALAND SOCIETY OF GENEALOGISTS   PO Box 8795, Auckland 3

REGISTRAR-GENERAL'S OFFICE   Private Bag, Lower Hutt

NEW ZEALAND FOUNDERS SOCIETY   PO Box 10 290, The Terrace, Wellington

NEW ZEALAND FAMILY HISTORY SOCIETY (formerly known as Armorial and Genealogical
    Institute)   PO Box 13301, Armagh, Christchurch

SOUTH AFRICA

GOVERNMENT ARCHIVES SERVICE   Union Building, Private Bag X236, Pretoria 0001

THE GENEALOGICAL SOCIETY   40 Haylett Street, Strand 7140
    Genealogical research undertaken for fee

INSTITUTE FOR GENEALOGICAL RESEARCH   The Human Sciences Research Council, Private
    Bag X41, Pretoria 0001

UNITED STATES OF AMERICA

There are innumerable genealogical societies in the United States, and no state is without one.
Addresses of those most likely to be able to help you in particular areas should be obtainable from one
of the two given below, or you can enquire at the library of the American Embassy in London.

NATIONAL ARCHIVES & RECORDS SERVICE   General Services Administration, Washington
    D.C., 20408
    Enquiries re military service, pension and passenger arrival records may be answered if sufficient
    detail is given and application made on official form
    Leaflet available describing holdings and conditions of search (Genealogical Records in the
    National Archives and Regional Branches of the National Archives)

GENEALOGICAL SOCIETY OF THE CHURCH OF JESUS CHRIST OF LATTER-DAY SAINTS   50 East
    North Temple, Salt Lake City, Utah 84150
    Holds film of statutory registration, parish and non-parochial records, public censuses, etc., for
    countries all over the world; large library of family and local history titles; genealogical serials;
    related publications; list of publications available

Index